Praise

*I Need To Know You: How to Meet Ordinary,
Extraordinary People and Improve Your Life*

"Kymberli Speight's *I Need To Know You* hooked me on the very first page! Her two guiding principles—*plant your crops before you're hungry* and *give without expectation*—are simple statements of networking 'best practices' that I've observed in the most effective networkers I've met in my 45-year career.

Although she started her journey doing something we're both passionate about—helping our fellow military veterans transition to their next phase—her lessons learned are priceless for anyone who wants to be a more effective networker.

Since her advice is clear, uncomplicated, and organized, you may be tempted to jump to her summaries—resist the urge! The stories she tells from her "100-day challenge" give her book heart that sets it apart from your typical "how-to" business book. This book isn't just a toolkit; it's a celebration of a rich and fulfilling life!"

—Darryl Scott
Maj Gen, USAF (Ret.)
President, MG DAS llc Consulting

"In *I Need To Know You*, Kymberli Speight reveals a simple yet elegant truth about networking: 'Meeting people becomes an easy behavior to adopt as a daily routine if you flip the focus from *what you can get* to **what you can give**.' Her insight and personal journey serve as a wonderful introduction to understanding how human connections can enrich our personal and professional lives."

—Rick Bailey
President of Northern New Mexico College
Co-Editor/Contributing Author to *Strategy:
Context and Adaptation from Archidamus
to Airpower*

"I followed Kymberli on Facebook during her challenge to meet 100 people in 100 days and found her new book to be a refreshing opportunity to observe how she initially met, interacted, and connected with people from very diverse backgrounds. She entered each interaction with a mindset of *what can I learn* and *how can I be of value to the people I meet*. Her detailed interactions and section on what she learned offer an interesting insight on how to build and sustain a strong network of professionals. I encourage anyone who is hesitant to network or wants to strengthen their network to read her book. Her formula for success is spot-on:

'Networking = Relationship Building = Building Social Capital + Being Mindful + Paying
Attention to Every Human Interaction'"

—Ed "Tank" McKinzie
Colonel, USAF (Ret.)
Business Development, Science & Technology

"In *I Need To Know You*, Kymberli Speight reminds us we don't just live in connection to others—we thrive! Each chapter tells a tale that encourages you to approach life open to the joy of a surprise and draw inspiration from conversation. As a lifelong introvert, I quietly read Kymberli's book as a vicarious extrovert; through her insights, conversational storytelling, and gentle encouragement, Kymberli reveals the secret to meeting ordinary, extraordinary people…"

—Derek Brown
Vice President, Major Accounts Manager

"*I Need To Know You* will help you understand 'how to be intentional about meeting people and cultivating relationships.' Kymberli is masterful in her ability to strike up a conversation with anyone, and she shares how you can do this too. Her creative use of words in her writing allows for visual pictures that will put you right into each encounter. She has successfully created deep and meaningful conversations with individuals due to her continued desire to learn and expand her circle of influence. If this book helps you make one additional meaningful connection, you will have succeeded in becoming a better version of yourself."

—Harlan Blumenthal
Toastmasters, past Area Director
Sr. Software Sales Executive

"I Need To Know You speaks to our heartaches. Connection to others is what we want and need. Kymberli bravely shows us how to lovingly ask and receive relatable, beautiful stories in the most eager places. I've watched her impromptu interviews, and the connections she makes in rare moments are told in these chapters of amazing love and adoration. We all should exemplify her."

—Patrick L. Reznik
Attorney, Counselor and Mediator

"With a healthy balance of inspiring stories and practical, actionable tips, *I Need To Know You* is a must-read resource if you struggle with networking like I do. There's no one-size-fits-all approach here, and I found myself identifying with and learning from many of the real-life stories."

—Marie Zimenoff
CEO, Career Thought Leaders and Resume
Writing Academy

I NEED TO KNOW YOU

HOW TO MEET ORDINARY, EXTRAORDINARY PEOPLE AND IMPROVE YOUR LIFE

KYMBERLI S.J. SPEIGHT

Printed in the United States of America

Published by Author Academy Elite

P.O. Box 43, Powell, OH 43035

Identifiers:
Paperback ISBN: 978-1-64085-761-2
Hardback ISBN: 978-1-64085-762-9
Ebook ISBN: 978-1-64085-763-6

Available in paperback, hardback, e-book, and audiobook

Library of Congress Control Number: 2019909226

Book design by Jetlaunch.
Cover design by Ryan Boire. EQN art by Dillon Speight.

DEDICATION

For all of the ordinary, extraordinary people out there. You are valuable, and your story is too!

In loving memory of my father, Sterling A. Johnson, Sr., who was a master networker and the first to show me the value of relationships and the importance of a smile.

In loving memory of my sister, Deidre K. Johnson. It was a gift to have her in my life for the time God allowed. I am thankful.

CONTENTS

PART 1: THEIR STORIES

PART 2: NETWORKING IS BUILDING RELATIONSHIPS

ACKNOWLEDGMENTS

It is with deep gratitude that I humbly offer my thanks to the people who generously gave of themselves and their time to help this book come to fruition. It has truly been a collective effort of ordinary yet extraordinary people. Thank you to...

My husband, Joel, for your love and support through this entire project. Thank you for your wise counsel and input in the editing process. You are the wind beneath my wings, and I love and respect you greatly.

My sons, Dustin and Dillon, for helping me to be a better person, teaching me how to love better and holding me accountable along the way. As adults now, you continue to teach me many things.

My mom for giving me life, loving me, and always being supportive.

My brother, Eddie. You were in daily contact with me during the time of my challenge, and you encouraged me.

Those of you I met. You are fearfully and wonderfully made. I treasure the time you spent with me, sharing a part of yourself.

You may never know how your personal story encourages someone else.

Everyone who cheered me on. Whether it was on Facebook, over the phone, or in person, I needed your support, and you came through every time. It amazes me how a little encouragement can truly go a long way. When I felt the world saying, "No, you can't. Who do you think you are?" you said, "Yes, you can." Together we did.

My friends that went above and beyond and introduced me to someone you knew. You demonstrated unselfish giving, too, as your extraordinary story was not being told. You were vital to the success of this project!

Harlan for giving me the right nudge at the right time.

My sister, Karmen, for insisting that I make 100 postings and not take the easy way out. Your persistence made for a much more robust book and personal journey.

Marguerite for coaching me on the structure for my book and your strong suggestion that I take the time and care these stories deserved. You showed me how I could make it so much better than I initially envisioned.

Amy for telling me the truth about my original title and for your time, expertise, and insight on the process of book publishing.

My editors, Kali and Gailyc. You both challenged me to flush out the details, and you helped me to say it with clarity. You offered fresh perspectives, and you each took it to the next level.

My brother, Buddy. You shared invaluable wisdom on my cover design from a marketing perspective. In a time of indecision, you provided knowledge and expertise, which produced clarity.

Bruce, Reggie, Leon, and Dave for taking the time to read my manuscript and letting me know it was worth pursuing. Thank you for your inputs as well. It helped shape my final product.

General Scott, Rick, Ed, Derek, Harlan, Patrick, and Marie for your generous endorsements.

Sandy Fitzgerald and Laura Norton for helping me edit the after print copy.

All those who are participating in the grassroots effort to get these stories out into the world—stories I know will touch the heart of the reader. They are a part of our collective history.

WHY THE 100-DAY CHALLENGE?

Why the 100-day challenge? Why not? It sounded like a great adventure! I got the idea when I attended a freelance conference in Austin. One of the presentations was by a bright and energetic woman named Keisha Mabry, who spoke about making connections. During her presentation, she shared that she had challenged herself to meet 100 people in 100 days when she moved to a new place.

This idea resonated with me because I give keynote speeches on networking and relationship building, and I coach individual clients who want to get better at it for both personal and professional reasons. I also teach a four-day executive transition seminar for military leaders who have served twenty to thirty years and are making plans to exit the military profession and enter the civilian market and way of life.

Many of those leaving the military will relocate to areas where they know a limited number of people while simultaneously looking for civilian work. Naturally, one of the things I emphasize in the transition course is learning to be an effective networker, because in most cases, the top-shelf job opportunities will only be discovered through networking.

What I found is that many people approach networking with a "what can I get" attitude. When I teach networking, I approach it from the perspective of "what can I give," and I focus on relationship building. I teach individuals how to meet people, create great conversations, and then develop those initial interactions into relationships. The 100 people, 100-day challenge was an effective way to add credibility to two concepts I often teach: plant your crops before you're hungry and give without expectation. I'm a firm believer that you will reap what you sow. It will come back to you, but it may not come back from where you initially planted the seeds. The truth is your network is your net worth. To my students who desperately need to expand their network, I wanted to be able to say, "If I can meet 100 people in 100 days, surely you can go out and meet fifteen to twenty new people." (I will say the same thing to you reading this book.) That is how my journey began.

Knowing that I like to do what I say I'm going to do, I thought I would add the accountability factor of telling my Facebook friends about my challenge. I told them that if the people I met allowed me to, I would take a picture. People were so gracious that they not only permitted me to take their picture, but they also shared a part of their stories with me and allowed me to post them on Facebook—and now include their stories in this book, which is the product of that work.

Most of the people I met were those I came into contact with while going about my daily life. Many were people I met within a fifteen-mile radius of my home. In each story, I share how that person came into my life or how the conversation began. I loved this journey and grew in so many ways. I hope their stories touch your heart as they did mine and inspire you to get more connected in your community.

What can you hope to gain by reading this book? Often, I hear people say they don't know how to expand their circle. More than once, someone has told me they didn't know their next-door neighbor but would like to, or that they are new to the area and don't know many people. Until I learned how to be intentional about meeting people and cultivating relationships, I didn't have an effective network. Now I have a vibrant network of friends and colleagues with whom I enjoy associating, which also keeps me connected to speaking and coaching opportunities. Simply stated, we need each other; I am convinced of this truth. We were not created to live life alone. We all crave connection. But as our society has evolved, busy schedules, job relocations, perceived differences, social media channels, and political disparities make it more challenging than ever to connect with others in a real and meaningful way.

Truly, I hope many of the stories in *I Need To Know You* will encourage and inspire you. However, I have also included essential principles and techniques on how to establish, grow, and nurture thriving networks that will benefit you both personally and professionally.

Here are some principles and techniques you will learn:

- Fundamentals of growing your network at any time

- Keys to networking and relationship building

- Techniques for having exceptional and memorable conversations

- Approaches for uncovering opportunities to give and receive help

- Ideas for meeting people

1

To My Surprise

To quote a most unexpected yet beautiful vocalist:
"Surprise! Surprise! Surprise!"

—Jim Nabors, aka Gomer Pyle

I met some of the most interesting people on my journey, and I would be rewarded time and time again with wonderful surprise gems. It was like being a kid eating a box of Cracker Jacks for the very first time and stumbling on the surprise inside because you didn't know it came with one; or on a summer day grabbing a box of cereal that contained a toy inside and you didn't know it would be you instead of your sibling finding it, but when you reached in, you were delighted beyond measure.

Life is full of surprises. Often they are good and yes, sometimes not so good. The stories you are about to read fall on the positive surprise side—they all contain an element of "Wow, I didn't expect to hear that!" The stories I heard opened my mind to the possibility of expanding my horizons and to questioning my limiting beliefs. They inspired me to step out of my comfort zone and to see myself and others differently. They beg the question, why do we spend time idolizing the movie star as if they are the only ones with an exciting life and a story to tell?

All of our stories have value. Our forefathers—no matter from what continent they hailed—knew this. Even before written language, they told their stories around the campfire. They told them to educate, to celebrate, to communicate. Who could benefit from hearing your story? What surprises might you discover if you pause to listen to another's story?

I thought it was appropriate to start with Keisha's story. I made myself travel an hour across town to attend my first session of the Freelance Conference (#FreeCon). I tell you this because if you're like me, traveling an hour away does not sound like fun, especially when going to hear someone speak you've never heard of before. Keisha spoke on the subject of connecting, which is something I am passionate about, so I went to see if I would learn anything new. When I arrived, I thought I would put what I teach about networking into practice, so I started approaching total strangers to start a conversation. After I made my way to the refreshment table and met a couple of people, I continued on my way back towards the room where the first presentation was to be held.

As I approached the meeting room, I saw two people standing by a table talking. Since they were standing at a ninety-degree angle to one another, I took it as a sign that they were open to someone else joining the conversation. I approached them, and like many times before, I introduced myself and started a conversation. I made some polite inquiries, and our discussion was developing nicely. Notice, I didn't start with the age-old question about what you do, which is both boring and predictable. Eventually, I did ask each of them, but only in general terms. Many initial conversations don't have to include the job question at all. I was interested in learning about each of them, and it wasn't until it was getting very close to start time that the event organizer approached us to speak to Elijah and Keisha.

Elijah happened to be one of the event coordinators, and Keisha, well, she turned out to be our guest speaker! Today, if I were going to an event, I would pay much more attention to the list of attendees as well as the featured speaker before going, but I hadn't done that. What I found out about Keisha during our chat was that she not only speaks on connecting but also personal branding. Ah-ha! We had a lot in common. As a side note, Elijah specialized in branding, too, so we spent most of our time chatting about where everyone was from and how they got into branding. I was asking the questions as my goal was to be curious, so I mainly listened.

Keisha started her presentation with an exuberant "Hey, friends!" She gave such an inspiring speech I was moved to take her 100-Day challenge. I bought her book called—wait for it—*Hey Friend*. Yes, that's the title! (It is an excellent book by the way.) I got quite a few tips from her book that I later used in my challenge, so I would say it was definitely worth the hour trip across town. What's even better is that Keisha and I have started to develop a relationship, and she was one of my biggest cheerleaders throughout my journey. Keisha and I are Facebook friends, so I can tell you that one of the things I have grown to love about her is that she gives generously to her network without any expectation of anything in return from a particular person. I love this about her because this approach aligns with my values and the way I teach networking.

I believe our lives are more vibrant when we are positively impacting others, and Keisha has undeniably influenced mine. Please, meet Keisha.

I met Joel at the Sententia Vera Cultural Hub in Dripping Springs. The Hub is a wonderful co-working space, book store, and coffee shop that has a mission to foster communication and engagement between languages and cultures. Joel was at the Hub to pick up a few yard signs for the upcoming midterm elections. One of the very first things he shared with me was that one of his ancestors died in the Battle of Franklin fighting for the Confederate army; I wasn't expecting that! Joel said it's possible to acknowledge his family's heritage and yet not carry their flag. He elaborated further and disclosed that his views are very different from theirs. Yes, this perfect stranger and I talked about two incredibly taboo subjects: politics and religion. I agreed with many of his views, and some I did not, but the great thing was we had an enjoyable conversation.

Joel has lived in Dripping Springs since 2006. He moved from Houston and has a lot of parrots in his aviary and at least three dogs. Joel started liking parrots when he was a teenager; he cultivated this affection on his first job while working in a pet store. In addition to owning parrots, Joel helps out at his friend's aviary where they have thousands of parrots.

One of Joel's hobbies is researching his genealogy. He actually found a court documented marriage certificate for one of his ancestors dating back to 1580! Professionally, Joel works for a title insurance company and is a digital guru. We must have talked for half an hour. What a treat it was to make his acquaintance! Please, meet Joel.

I had the pleasure of meeting another guest speaker, Candice, at the Freelance Conference. She spoke on a different day. Her topic was, "Find Your Tribe: A Guide to Effective Market Research." Candice is very knowledgeable about market research, so I thought it would be good to reach out to her on LinkedIn and invite her to connect. Not only did she connect with me, but she also sent a warm message back. We developed a dialogue, and she asked me to tell her more about what I did. We decided to meet in person to get to know one another better, and I am so glad I did. Her story fascinated me!

Candice grew up in New York and got a degree in music management. Okay, that was unexpected given what I knew about her up to this point! She started out working as a band manager but found many musicians to be high maintenance. The rumors are true; some people demand their M&M's be separated by color! Finding herself doing this very task, Candice decided to move on to other things. Marketing caught her eye. Before she made her career move though, she did get to meet Aretha Franklin and B.B. King! As she shared this, I remember feeling amazed; I grew up listening to their music, but somehow, the idea of ever meeting either one of them seemed out of the realm of possibility. Another fun fact Candice shared was that she also worked at Carnegie Hall!

Candice relocated to Austin where she met and married her husband, Jeff, who is a video editor. She is an organized creative and has an "I can do it, you'll see!" attitude. Today, she runs Beckmann Collaborative, a business training and marketing consulting firm for small businesses that focuses on marketing operations and marketing strategy. Her experience includes strategy, marketing campaigns, content creation, relationship management, grassroots marketing, barter marketing, guerrilla marketing, events, and market research. If you need help in any of these areas, check out her website at https://BeckmannCollaborative.com/.

Candice still enjoys getting back to her musical roots and is a member of the Austin Harmony Chorus, which is a women's a cappella barbershop chorus group that not only performs but competes. Candice invited me to their Veteran's Day Concert, which was quite lovely, and I was able to meet Jeff. Please, meet Candice.

I met Daeric totally by happenstance. I was shopping at a favorite Texas grocery store, HEB, and headed to the checkout when I noticed Daeric coming in the opposite direction. Actually what caught my eye was his blue t-shirt that had big white letters that read CAPE MAY; I wish I had captured more of his shirt in the picture.

Cape May is in the southern part of New Jersey, and it is where I spent every summer from birth until I left for college. As he approached, I said, "Have you ever been to Cape May, or are you just wearing the t-shirt?"

He said he had been there and still goes there about every other year. His wife makes it there every year. Now I was intrigued! Since moving to Texas, I seldom get to Cape May even though I have such fond memories of being at the shore as a kid. My mom still owns a home there. Daeric told me he stays at one of the houses across from the Victoria, a place I know quite well.

Daeric is from Waco but worked in Pennsylvania for a year. He is an IT Solutions consultant. I am curious about the origins of the spelling of his name. His wife's family lives in Temple, Texas, but is originally from Pennsylvania. Her family regularly vacationed in Cape May and introduced Daeric to this great place. Daeric said he now loves the beach and enjoys family vacations there. What a delightful coincidence! Please, meet Daeric.

Anthony came to my home to change out my TV service. He had been working for over an hour while I was also working. Somewhere in the recesses of my mind, I heard, "Ask Anthony if he will share his story with you." So I did, and he agreed.

Anthony exudes an easy-going personality. He was born in San Antonio and lived in South Carolina and Houston before moving to Austin on Halloween of 2000. He likes it here, so he has stayed put. He said after high school he was flying by the seat of his pants until his girlfriend told him about a job installing TV services. He has been installing TVs for the past fifteen years and thoroughly enjoys it, meeting anywhere from five to ten customers every day. There could be two adults at the house plus kids. He said you never know what you are walking into— happy people, cranky people, shy people. I asked Anthony who his most interesting customer was.

Anthony said, "Dennis Quaid."

"What?" I was flabbergasted.

Anthony said he got his work order for the job in the morning, and it had the wife's name on it. He joked with his boss that it was Dennis Quaid's house, not actually believing it was. Anthony called the number to let the customer know when he would arrive. He told me that when he showed up, Mrs. Quaid started walking him around, then stopped and said, "You know, this is my husband's baby. Let him handle it." She called out, "Dennis!"

Anthony said he thought to himself, "No way!" He said he turned around and standing five feet away from him was Dennis Quaid. They spent the next four hours walking around figuring out where Dennis wanted his boxes. Anthony said Dennis (you know, I'm on a first-name basis with him myself) was very down to earth; very realistic and straightforward.

I asked him who his most difficult customer was. Joking, I said, "Please don't say it was me!"

He said he doesn't have difficult customers, only tricky situations. He shared that sometimes you can't get a cable exactly where the customer wants it: challenging circumstances, but not difficult customers. Great perspective in his line of work, don't you think?

Anthony has several hobbies he enjoys. He is a drummer and likes playing the drums to rock music. He used to be in a band that played gigs out; now they just jam. When he is at home, he often turns up the stereo really loud and plays along. Anthony lives out in the country, so he is not disturbing anyone. He is also a cook, a carpenter, and an artist.

Anthony says he draws a lot, but his favorite hobby seems to be cooking. He can come home from working a ten-hour shift and whip up something delicious. He actually said, "It's fun!"

I told him cooking and fun are *not* two words I would use in the same sentence. He suggested I try to explore using different seasonings and spices and that if it didn't taste good, I should keep experimenting. That does not sound like fun to me, but hey, different strokes for different folks!

Anthony has three brothers and a sister. He enjoys being an uncle—except when the children break his stuff. He said he learns as much from them as he teaches them and hopes to be a dad one day. He is engaged, so that may not be eons away. Please, meet Anthony.

The day I met Steve, he was extremely excited. I had just gotten in line to vote in the midterm elections when Steve walked up behind me exuding an abundance of energy. He told me within the first twenty-eight seconds of our meeting the cause for his exuberance—this was the first time Steve was eligible to vote, but before he did, I got his story.

Steve moved to Austin in 2010 from Montreal, where he was born and raised. His father was Greek, and his mother was from France; so he was able to speak three languages fluently from the age of three. Steve said he always had a zest for life and exploration, so he left Montreal when he was twenty-five and moved to Calgary (a city in Alberta, Canada near the Rocky Mountains). He lived there and skied, as well as other fun things. Carefree, he moved to Toronto and found a job doing project management. That job brought him to Austin.

Steve said he moved to Austin with no car, no furniture, no house, and no belongings. He only had his clothes, his computer, a TV and his hockey bag. Eight years later, Steve has a wife, two kids, a house, a black (not white) picket fence, two cars, and a job. He said he was living the American dream and fulfilling the dream today by voting. He was genuinely excited, which was nice to see. He was taking his civic duty seriously and counted it a privilege to vote.

I asked him if he goes back to Montreal to visit. He does about every two to three years, but he no longer has any immediate family living there. He plans to go back next Christmas because it is gorgeous there with the snow and pine trees, and he wants his children to experience that. I asked him if he was going to teach his children other languages since he speaks three. He told me he speaks to his son only in Greek and to his daughter solely in French. His wife is Russian (also a U.S. citizen now), so she speaks to the children in Russian. He and his wife talk to each other in English. The plan is that both children will grow up knowing four different languages; now that's what I call multi-lingual. What a gift!

Steve just finished his MBA at Pepperdine University. He said it took him fifteen months, and he had to attend a class in California for nineteen weekends. I think that's pretty impressive; anyone who goes back to school while having young children is a serious multi-tasker, or their spouses are superheroes. It can only be one or the other or some combination of the two.

Steve seems to me to be Type A. His next goal is to write an all-encompassing book with a partner based on his MBA studies and focused on helping new employees succeed in the workplace after their first ninety days. His goal is to complete the first chapter in the next two weeks.

I asked him if he has any hobbies. He said he likes to play hockey and golf. When I asked if he'd like to share anything else, he said, "Standing in line to vote is really annoying. Standing here, talking to another fun person (uh…that would be me) is a great way to pass the time and a great way to meet someone new."

Steve liked my challenge. In his words, he thought it was "amazing." I would have to agree with him. I was meeting some pretty fabulous and adventurous people! He's one for sure. Please, meet Steve.

I took my car in to the dealership to get it washed, so I had some time to kill. I ran into Donovan and Lester. I will tell you about Donovan today and introduce you to Lester in Chapter 7, where I will touch on giving.

Donovan is a young man who was waiting to have his car washed too. As I walked over to the waiting area, he looked up and welcomed me with a big smile on his face: a warm, welcoming smile. I liked him immediately. He asked me how my day was going, and of course, that is all it took; by now, you know I am determined to meet someone new.

Donovan was born in Fresno, California. His family moved to Venezuela, where his father's family is from, when he was two months old. He lived there until he was a freshman in high school. At that time they moved to Austin, where his mother's family originated. His mother's family has lived in Austin for five generations and more than 150 years; this is pretty significant as most people I run into are transplants to Austin. As you might imagine, moving from Venezuela to Austin was quite a change for Donovan. Venezuela was, of course, much more tropical, but already speaking Spanish was reasonably helpful, I'm sure.

When I asked him what he did for a living, he jokingly replied, "Generally as little as possible!" Then he confessed he has a few jobs. He is very entrepreneur-minded. Donovan is a GM for a small for-profit organization, a partner in a team-building and outdoor recreation business called Bound Outdoors (http://boundoutdoors.com), and a partner in another business venture as well. For one so young, I was not expecting to hear that, but I've learned to expect the unexpected. I asked him what the pull was to the Bound Outdoors business. He told me he used to be a river guide for several years, and that was the impetus for starting the company.

Donovan has a younger brother and sister and two feral cats that he shared are not particularly friendly. I found out he enjoys playing soccer and gardening. Now soccer I can see, but I wouldn't have guessed gardening. Just when we would have started chatting about the best types of fertilizers, Mark, my service rep, came with the keys to my car. Talking to Donovan made my wait go by super-fast. He has a delightful personality. Please, meet Donovan.

Kristin and Madison are a great mom-daughter duo. Kristin is joining our volunteer coffee team at church, and I was training her to do tear-down (washing the pots and putting all the coffee/tea condiments away): she is a fast learner. Her daughter, Madison, was willing to help out too.

Kristin is from San Antonio and moved to Austin when she got married twenty-one years ago. She has three stepbrothers and one sister. Kristen enjoys running, working out, reading, and time with family. Her grandparents and mom have been in the education field. With that influence in her life, Kristin has wanted to be a teacher as long as she can remember. Kristin set teaching as a goal, and that's what she did right out of college. She taught special education and general education. After becoming a mom, though, Kristin took off a few years. When she was ready to return to the workforce, she took a slightly different path and became the preschool director at a church for six years.

Kristin eventually realized she missed being in the classroom and returned to her true love of teaching four years ago. When she first left teaching, film strips were in fashion (and we all know technology has moved way past that). Kristin embraced the new technology by taking a few classes, but she credits her students the most with keeping her up-to-date with the latest technology. Teaching is her dream job, and she is thrilled with where she is now in her career.

Kristin has two children, Madison, who is sixteen and a junior in high school, and Walker, who is thirteen and an eighth grader. Kristin's daughter, Madison, is already an entrepreneur; she uses watercolor to paint paper goods like stationery and bible covers. Madison became interested in watercolor painting two years ago. She learned fast, and soon her friends were asking her to paint things for them. Madison started painting stationary and then included prayer journals and bibles as a way to share the gospel. She had an Instagram account for her business to get the word out. Low and behold, a company in Grapevine, Texas, saw her work and is now placing orders with her. You can find her art on Instagram at @mlwrighting.

Madison's favorite subjects in school are history or English— depending on the teacher. This year she said she has a lot of great teachers but is taking many challenging courses. Looking toward her future, she thinks she would like to do graphic design or marketing. Madison has excellent resume content already, no matter which path she chooses. She hopes to attend Texas A & M since that is where both of her parents went, and she likes the community and tradition there.

Wise beyond her years, Madison told me she is, "trying to find joy in the simple things." She mentioned she was getting baptized the following week and was excited about that. Madison is also challenging herself by reading the entire Bible. She did admit that the book of Numbers is hard to get through because it is on the Law, but she is determined. She strikes me as the type of person that will accomplish what she sets out to do. Please, Meet Kristin and Madison.

It was a beautiful, sunny day after several not-so-nice cold and overcast days when I decided to take a drive into town, and I passed by our local farmer's market. Sometimes I stop, but often I'm in a hurry, so I drive right by it because I'm on my way somewhere. That day I thought it might be a great place to meet someone. I was correct. I met Laurel, and I had the most delightful conversation with her.

Laurel is a native "Austinite" and is a graduate of the University of Texas with a degree in radio, television, and film. She worked in that area for a short time but followed her culinary passion and went to work in a couple of bakeries as a cake decorator and baker. Then Laurel went back to school; this time, she went to Los Angeles to get a degree in pastry and baking. She has worked in Los Angeles, New York City, and now is back in Austin.

Laurel is an entrepreneur at heart. She has tried other businesses but did not hang on to those. You know what they say—if at first, you don't succeed, try, try again. Six months ago she had another idea, and this time it was a hit. She became a vendor at the Buda Farmer's market, selling her very own family recipe for granola when Buda expanded their vendor list. She thought it would be fun. Years ago, she created an almond-coconut granola recipe for her family when she could not find organic, low sugar granola in the stores. It was a hit with her family. They loved it, and it turns out, the Buda community did too! Her business has been growing ever since; she is now in several local health food stores. I can tell you from experience why. It is indeed delicious, and I don't think I've tasted better granola in recent memory.

I am neither a foodie nor a granola lover, but I must tell you, I had a hard time putting Laurel's granola down! It was a taste bud revelation. I was mad at myself because I wanted to take a picture of it with all of its apple pieces (that in and of itself is odd because I don't generally take pictures of food), but I ate most of them before I got home. Anyway, you can see some of what was left in the picture. The tastes of wholesomeness (whatever that is) and flavor, were bursting in my mouth.

Back to Laurel. She is married and has a seven-year-old son. Her hobbies are writing, reading (mysteries as well as books on food and nutrition), and running. She ran a marathon in May. I have never run more than three miles myself, so I'm duly impressed with her physical stamina!

I asked her if there was anything else she wanted to share. Laurel told me she's almost forty, and it took her this long to figure out she could do something she loves and earn a living at it. After all, she had been working twenty years full-time for other people's dreams until she launched hers. She said, "Thinking about it, and reading about it, and writing about it is helpful, but if you don't actually just do it, then you're never going to. If I can do it, honestly, then anybody else can too."

Laurel makes it look easy now, but her story truly exemplifies the saying, "When preparation meets opportunity." She has a good product, has worked in management in Whole Foods and other bakeries, too, and knew a little about packaging and logistics. If you want to try her granola, you can find her at http://www. laurelsfarmhousemarket.com. Please, meet Laurel.

I would like to introduce you to Kade. He is the third person I met at one coffee shop all on the same day. I had just finished getting Parker's story, whom I will introduce you to in Chapter 2 and was returning to the communal table when Kade looked up and smiled. I hesitated for a moment, then I complimented him on having a friendly smile, and our conversation began.

Kade is an only child and originally from Dallas. He moved to Austin to attend the University of Texas, where he studied finance. I told him a little about how my challenge came about. That's when he told me his grandfather was in the Air Force before he went on to be the CFO of a company in Germany.

Kade is very business-oriented. He started his own landscaping company when he was thirteen. I don't know about you, but when I was that age, I may have cut a few lawns; but I didn't have a bigger picture in mind. He did. The company grew pretty large, and Kade ran it until he was twenty, at which time he employed a couple of his older family members to run it for him while he finished college.

When he came to Austin, Kade met two guys who were running a public investment partnership. He started working with them, making investments. One thing led to another, and the three of them decided to collaborate. Two years ago they convinced their investment partners to buy a large landscaping and construction company in Austin. Their logic, Kade said, "Because, why not?"

Kade graduated from the University of Texas in May of 2017. He and his two partners have been running this company since. They started with fifty-seven employees and are now approaching 250 employees. Kade said, "It's been a wild ride!"

In his spare time, Kade likes to travel. He has been to Rio de Janeiro, Brazil, Australia, and Spain. He also enjoys working out at the gym and hanging out with friends—you know—typical stuff. That day though, he was hanging out at the coffee shop working while he was waiting for one of his customer's Christmas parties to start; he was bringing them pies. We both agreed on the importance of relationship building. Please, meet Kade.

2

JUST GETTING STARTED

"Two roads diverged in a wood, and I—
I took the one less traveled by,
And that has made all the difference."

—Robert Frost

Your early twenties can be a great time in life. Yes, it is confusing, and you are trying to figure out which way to go, but there is also a sense that you can do anything, and you are just figuring it out for yourself. Somewhere along the line, we mature and take on additional heavy responsibilities: a spouse, children, perhaps a house. Life seems to get much more serious. It has always been serious, but more layers get added; the decisions we make will impact not only our future but the futures of those who are now relying on us.

Just because someone in their twenties is starting to venture out without having to live under the rules of their parents, it doesn't mean they have not encountered some hard things in life. It is just to say there is a sense about them that they are at a many-pronged road at which point they may make a multitude of choices. Trying to figure all of that out can be daunting, but day by day, they will rise to the challenge of making choices that will put them on their road less traveled. By definition, their road is less traveled, for only each person alone can make their particular journey.

I met Kris at Gold's Gym. He's an employee there and was checking people in when I came for my workout. Kris has the right type of personality for customer service; he is an amiable person with a great smile. He is a nineteen-year-old sophomore in college, pursuing a degree in criminal justice. Kris wants to be a lawyer and a part of the solution for the underserved. He moved from El Paso to Austin to be closer to his mom to help her and his younger siblings. I think he is the only young person I have met so far that is not on social media. I did encourage him to get on LinkedIn, though, to start building his professional network.

There were several great things about meeting Kris on this journey. Since I was posting these stories on Facebook, a couple of my friends who read his story were willing to help Kris—to mentor him, if you will. One of my friends who offered to help is a judge, and another is an attorney. What a wealth of knowledge they have to share, and I was happy to convey that information to him. The question is, will Kris reach out to them? Which road will he take? Will he go it alone, as many young people try initially, or will he take the risk to pick up the phone? I ask this question not to call Kris out, but for those of you reading. All too often, I work with job seekers, people in their thirties, forties, and older who hesitate to pick up the phone to ask for help by way of asking for information. I make the distinction here because if you are looking for work, you should avoid asking your friends for a job. Instead, many would love to provide help by way of actionable information; the specific help you need may be only one conversation away.

Now, getting back to Kris, it was great to find out later that Joey, whom I will introduce you to in Chapter 8, connected with Kris. Joey initiated the contact after reading Kris' story on my Facebook timeline. Since their initial meeting, they have had a couple of conversations. I think that is wonderful! Someone doesn't have to be in your same career field to mentor you or open up doors for you. It takes a while to get to know someone, so my philosophy is the sooner a person gets busy getting to know others, the better. You never know if they can help you down the road or if you can be of help to them. Please, meet Kris.

I would like to introduce you to Cayla. She is a recent high school graduate who works at a local coffee shop. She is presently taking community college courses but wants to go to Texas A&M to become a pediatrician. We all know that getting into medical school is not an easy task. Cayla will make countless decisions along the way: to study or not to study, that is the question. From what I know of her, though, I think she will choose to study.

The day I met Cayla, it was my Sunday to volunteer at the coffee table at church. When Cayla approached the table before service, she seemed to recognize me and asked me how I was doing. I told her, "Better than I deserve," which is always true.

It turns out Dave Ramsey says the same thing, and Cayla listens to his program. That says a lot about her right there. Don't you love her smile?

Interestingly enough, I had just bought a cup of coffee from Cayla the previous week, and then I saw her at church! Cayla looked familiar, but I couldn't remember where I had seen her. Normally I would have let this go, but because I was doing this challenge, I asked her where I had seen her. As soon as she reminded me, I immediately connected to the experience. She was super friendly then, too, as she had gone about her work making my coffee drink. While talking to her at church, I remember thinking, "*Hmm... Did I leave her a good tip?*" Ha! Thankfully, I think it was respectable.

I see Cayla all the time at church now. After posting her story, a friend who owns a petting zoo reached out to ask me if Cayla did house and pet sitting on the side. I was able to connect them. A win-win! Please, meet Cayla.

I met two fabulous young ladies, Jewelia and Alexis, educating the public about the D.A.R.E. program. D.A.R.E. stands for Drug Abuse Resistance Education. This program seeks to prevent the use of controlled drugs, membership in gangs, and violent behavior amongst students. The first D.A.R.E. program lacked statistical data to prove its worth, but it was revised in 2009 and now has proven its success. These two ladies were out fundraising because D.A.R.E. lost its federal funding, and they are working hard to get the program back into the schools. If you would like to read more about D.A.R.E. and what they have accomplished, you can visit https://dare.org/the-new-dare-program-this-one-works/.

Let me tell you a bit about Jewelia and Alexis. Jewelia is originally from New Mexico. She graduated from college a year ago with a degree in international studies in linguistics, then moved to San Antonio to be with her twelve-year-old little brother. Jewelia loves helping out kids and getting involved in the community, so working with the D.A.R.E. program was a perfect fit for her. Jewelia wants to work to put the program back in the schools, to make an impact, and to keep kids safe. Even though she is just getting started herself, she is already reaching back to help others attain a successful start in life. Please, meet Jewelia.

Alexis is currently going to college and is twenty-one years old. She is originally from Mississippi but has also lived in Jamaica and several Asian countries. Her major is international marketing with a focus on Asia. Both of her parents are lawyers, and she is quite proud of them. Alexis is multi-lingual and said she learns languages best by watching soap operas and then practicing with native speakers. Alexis had personal experience with D.A.R.E. when she was in school; she credits this program with educating her about drugs and arming her with the knowledge that if someone was trying to persuade her to try drugs, knowing what drugs do to you, that they were not her real friends. Alexis said she learned a true friend would not want you to take or do something that would be harmful to you. She is a smart young lady who has already made some wise decisions about her future. Please, meet Alexis.

My husband, Joel, and I were going to take a road trip, so we rented a car from Enterprise. Scott showed up at our door to pick us up to get our rental. He is in their leadership training program. Scott is very upbeat and is a relatively recent graduate of Texas State. Go Bobcats! He got his degree in business management. His younger sister graduated from Texas State, too.

Scott likes BBQ; no surprise there, as he is from Lockhart, TX, which he proudly told me is the BBQ capital of Texas. For all you BBQ fans, his favorite BBQ restaurant is Chisholm Trail because they have a great sauce. He is an Eagle Scout and credits the Boy Scouts with excellent leadership training. He said he is not afraid of taking charge of projects that need to get done in a collective environment.

I would say Scott is pretty fortunate. Why? Because he gets to go on brocations! He still gets together with his high school friends *and their dads* once a year for camping trips, BBQ cook-off challenges, and lots of other fun adventures. There are about nine of them who go, and they have been doing it since the ninth grade. To have long-lasting friends and mentors in one is a huge advantage! I think it is fantastic for men to have other men on whom they can count. Scott enjoys capturing these adventures on video or in pictures and produces a montage of their times together. It would be interesting to see if Scott and his friends continue this tradition when they have children.

Scott says he enjoys meeting new people daily and has terrific coworkers. An added perk is that he likes talking to his corporate customers and learning about their work. Speaking of work, I can appreciate his philosophy: "You put your head down and keep working." Even though he is all about getting the job done, there is another side to Scott: he has a pretty awesome sense of humor! As he was driving us up to the rental car place, he kept us laughing for most of the trip. Joel and I thoroughly enjoyed our conversation with him and appreciated his friendliness early in the morning. Please, meet Scott.

I met the nicest young lady working at the hotel where Joel and I were staying. Her name is Jocylen. First of all, I love the spelling of her name, though she told me she doesn't like her first name. She prefers her middle name, which is beautiful, too. It's Alazay. The first two a's have the "ah" sound. She is eighteen and plans to start college in January.

We talked a little about her future goals. She, like most young adults, is trying to figure out life; she has been very interested in the medical field ever since she was a little girl. The question for her at this point is, does she study medicine for humans or our furry friends?

Jocylen is pondering this question because of Bella. Bella is a one-year-old Shi-Tzu and toy poodle mix. She got Bella when she was a six-week-old puppy. Jocylen fondly remembers Bella hiding under the bed at first; but once she turned two and a half months, Bella would follow her everywhere she went! They have formed a very close allegiance now.

Jocylen is one of four children and is the only girl. She has a cousin around the same age, and they treat each other like sisters. This year, at such a young age, Jocylen experienced a personal loss—her twenty-one-year-old brother, Angel. She said she learned from that experience to take no one for granted. Her advice is always check in with those you love. She says that she is always saying hello where before she might not have, and she feels a deeper connection to people. She is wise beyond her years.

I know from personal experience that when tragedy strikes, life can become very confusing, but you must keep putting one foot in front of the other. Here is my new young friend—please, meet Jocylen and Bella.

Are you ready for another American Dream story? Then let me introduce you to Marvin. He works at the AT&T store where Joel and I were getting new iPhones, but we were assigned to another customer service representative. Marvin was kind enough to let me capture his story while we waited our turn.

Marvin was born in Germany to a German father and a Mexican mother. Their family immigrated to the United States when he was one. They moved to Florida then to South Texas. Marvin came to Austin five years ago to attend the University of Texas—he's a Longhorn fan. Marvin has a younger brother and a younger sister. His sister graduated from the University of Texas also. He is twenty-five years old and was pretty pumped about celebrating his upcoming birthday.

Marvin got his degree in public health. He hopes to make it big in nursing one day. Marvin plans to attend an alternate entry Master of Science & Nursing program to become a nurse. He has always been interested in the medical field; while he was growing up, he enjoyed watching *House*. He even took several medical classes in the dual enrollment program in high school. He told me his mom had always wanted to go into the medical field but wasn't able to. His mother grew up poor in Mexico, so she had to drop out of school when she was fifteen to help put her siblings through school. He shared with me that in a way, he will be living out her dream.

Marvin's hobbies include hanging out with friends and kickboxing. He has a puppy named Daenerys, named after the queen dragon on the show *Game of Thrones*. He calls her Daeni (Dani) for short. He said she doesn't behave as cute as she looks; in fact, he says she quite often misbehaves. He regularly takes her and her sister, who belongs to his roommate, to the park for walks.

Marvin is very proud of his father. He said when his dad got an opportunity, he took it. His dad is doing well for himself and now has a plumbing business. Marvin is a citizen of both the U.S. as well as Germany, and he speaks Spanish, German, and English. He is planning a trip back to Germany for the first time since he moved away as a baby. He is going back for his cousin's wedding and is excited to see where he was born. Please, meet Marvin and Daenerys.

I met Tanner at the AT&T store the same day I met Marvin. He was the customer service representative assigned to help us,

28

and I joined the conversation when he and Joel were discussing family genes: specifically the gene for baldness. Not sure how that came about because Tanner is only twenty-six. But, he did say baldness runs in his family.

There are five people in Tanner's immediate family: Mom, Dad, two brothers, and himself. Tanner is the tallest of the sons. I can tell you right now that he has a keen sense of humor. I was going to share with him what my dad used to say about bald heads, so I was starting to describe the hairline my father had when Tanner burst out, "The cul-de-sac!" He had me laughing hard! My dad used to say, "God only made a few perfect heads— on the rest, He put hair."

Getting back to Tanner, he can multitask well. He effortlessly set up our new phones while engaging in very entertaining conversation. He has a goal of gaining twenty-five pounds in the next year because he has always been tall and thin; Tanner shared that he doesn't want to be bald and skinny! He also wants to grow a beard. According to him, bald is in, but it looks even better with a beard. Evidently, he has really given this some thought.

Tanner is originally from Middleton, Texas, but grew up in South Dallas. After a year at Blinn College, he realized he wasn't quite ready for it, so he went back home and attended community college to get the basics done. Tanner decided, at that point, to pause to figure out what he wants to do. He has been working here in Austin for the past five months.

Tanner enjoys sales because it allows him to interact with people and connect with his customers on different levels. As he considers his options, he is leaning towards teaching or counseling and wants to study psychology; he wants to get involved with the younger generation.

Over the next year, Tanner plans to explore a lot of new things. He wants to learn to play the piano and get into photography. He also realizes he values real photos over the digital ones, so he has purchased a Polaroid camera to experiment. Tanner is very self-aware and feels like he is making progress in his life. Some of his favorite activities are meditation, yoga, and watching sports.

He is excited about his "growth year" as he calls it. Please, meet Tanner.

I had the pleasure of running into an inspiring young lady named Victoria on a trip to our local grocery store, HEB, to buy printer paper. As I was leaving the store, my eyes locked on to a Washington, D.C., sweatshirt. Being from that area of the country, I was curious to meet someone who might be a fellow east coaster. I turned and called out to her, making a reference to her sweatshirt. She told me she was not from D.C. but had visited there in August and thought it was great. I mentioned that I was from the D.C. area and then told her about my challenge. She was a terrific sport and agreed to participate.

Victoria is from Corpus Christi and is the youngest of four children. She has two older brothers, ages twenty-three and almost twenty-one, and a sister aged nineteen. Her family moved to Austin when she was six to send her sister to the Texas School for the Deaf. This year, Victoria is a senior in high school and has plans to attend the Gallaudet University in Washington, D.C. in the fall. Gallaudet University is a federally chartered, private university for the education of the deaf and hearing-impaired. Inspired by her sister, to whom she is very close, Victoria wants to become an interpreter to be able to help people with hearing issues communicate.

Victoria was all smiles. It turns out she was not coming to HEB to shop; she works there. I had never seen her before, but she told me she works there a lot. As we chatted, I found out her favorite class in school is a toss-up between English and Wildlife & Fisheries. She is the type of person who is very concerned about others and our environment. Like most young people, she enjoys listening to music and hanging out with friends. Victoria has a soft spot for furry friends too; she has two Chihuahuas and a Yorkie. I asked her if there was anything else she wanted to share, and she told me she thinks this challenge is pretty awesome.

What I found to be a delight were the many unsolicited comments posted on my timeline by her family and friends—comments like "We love Victoria. She's a hardworking and an amazing human. Glad she's part of our family." That spoke volumes to me about who Victoria is as a person beyond our initial meeting. That speaks volumes to an employer too; nowadays, many hiring officials will interview references in much the same way they do a job seeker, or they will go to their back channel to see what their network is saying about a particular candidate, especially when it comes to more senior roles. My litmus test has long been what a person's family and friends say about them. If you listen carefully, you will hear the truth, even in their jokes. Victoria would pass that test with flying colors. Please, meet Victoria.

I hit the jackpot. I met three people in one afternoon and all in one location—at a coffee shop on the outskirts of Austin. I had just come from the gym and had an appointment scheduled in a couple of hours. I could have gone back home; instead, I thought I would go to the coffee shop to work on a speech. I sat at a communal table in case the opportunity presented itself to start a conversation; it didn't. After a while, Cayla, whom I already told you about, walked in. It was nice to see her again. She was there working on a project for class, and of course, I was on my usual mission to meet people. To help make this happen, Cayla called up a friend of hers, Jake. Jake stopped what he was doing and came to the coffee house to help out his friend, Cayla. Jake was the first of the three people I was going to meet.

(Side-note: It is often a friend of a friend from whence cometh your help—whether it be learning of a job opportunity, a business opportunity, or just random support.)

Jake was raised on the outskirts of Austin, near Dripping Springs, and has two sisters. After high school, he went to college for a while but came back home to work. He worked on water wells for a while and found that to be very interesting; he enjoyed learning about the wells and how PVC pipes went together.

Overall, Jake likes learning new things, but not in a "school" environment. He discovered he prefers working with his hands.

Jake likes talking to people, learning about different cultures, and how people live. For instance, he told me about a family trip up the east coast to Canada and the people he met. Along the way, he particularly loved seeing Maine in the fall and visiting the national parks in the area. One thing that jumped out at him was that on the east coast, there are no HEB stores, which are prevalent in Texas. Sacrilege!

Jake's family lives on ten acres above a bend in Barton Creek with a great view of the creek; he thinks it's quite beautiful. Because he lives out in the country, he has recently acquired three outside kittens. Yes, I did say "outside" kittens. He says most city folks think it's weird to have "outside" kittens, but that's because they don't understand country living. Please, meet Jake.

Parker was the second of three people I met at the coffee shop that day. (I already told you about the third person, Kade, in Chapter 1.) I had initially asked Parker's co-worker if I could get his story. He was a bit shy, so he yelled to someone in the backroom to see if the person back there was up for the challenge. You guessed it; the person in the back was Parker. Because he was working, I waited until there was a lull before we started our conversation.

Parker is originally from Austin and is the youngest of four siblings who were all homeschooled at some point in their academic careers. His parents emphasized not wasting time and focusing on what he was genuinely interested in pursuing. For Parker, that was music. He was influenced by his father's band called The Antelope that performed in the early seventies. I don't think the group made it big, but they sure made an impression on young Parker, who fell in love with the drums at the age of five. Parker started playing music at the age of nine when he found his father's keyboard in the garage and began teaching himself to play it.

Now that he is older, Parker wants to focus on the more technical side of music. He wants to work in a studio and has plans to open up a recording studio eventually. In addition to working at the coffee shop, Parker has been amassing equipment to put together his home studio. He has been working diligently on producing a record for the last two years. Eventually, he would love to help other artists record. The part about recording that fascinates him the most is the intersection between music and physics—controlling the acoustics of it. He finds it empowering to have the ability to "engage" with wavelengths going through the air to "shape that sound" so people can experience it the way the artist intends.

His biggest challenge, as it is for many artists, is being a perfectionist. Talking with him left me with the impression that he is extremely creative and is bound to follow his dreams. Please, meet Parker.

I was introduced to Thy, pronounced TEE by a young lady named Ari. You will meet Ari later in Chapter 9. Thy is originally from Vietnam and moved to the United States with her family when she was three and a half years old. She has an older brother and an older sister. Thy claims Houston as her home since she lived there for ten years, and that is where her family lives; she goes home whenever she can and loves spending time with them. Currently, Thy is attending Texas State and working in Austin. She is studying nursing and biology with the hope of going to medical school one day and becoming a hematologist.

On a follow-up visit to Baskin Robbins to get my favorite ice cream, chocolate chip, I saw both Ari and Thy again, and they both remembered me. While I was catching up with them, I asked Thy why she was interested in hematology in particular. I thought there was perhaps some dramatic reason from her past, but what she said just made total sense; it's something she believes she would be good at. It's just that simple and logical. She realized she is not squeamish about the sight of blood, as many other people are. When her mom or someone needs help, and there is blood involved, she's the first one to help. Where other people may faint at the sight of blood, she thinks, "Ooh—let me see!" As a career coach, I love it when people can follow their passions and interests professionally.

Have you ever stopped to think about what it would take to pursue a specialty like hematology? I was curious about the training required, so I looked into it. Thy will need to attend four years of medical school after her undergraduate. She will then have three years of residency, followed by two to four years for a fellowship to gain expertise in a subspecialty; that's a lot of schooling, but I know she can do it. Thy will undoubtedly have a lot of decisions to make along the way.

Thy loves to dance. She danced for four years while in high school. Get this—she was able to dance in Super Bowl LI—the one at which Lady Gaga performed in Houston. She told me it is her favorite memory of all time. "It was amazing!" She wasn't on stage but performed with her high school drill team in the crowd. They practiced for weeks on end, and no one could know—not her teachers, not her friends, not even her parents. It was all so secretive, but she said when she thinks of it, that's her happy place. In addition to dancing, she likes to paint, to do arts and crafts, and to be outdoors. Please, meet Thy.

My friend, Megan, introduced me to her friend, Matt. He and his brother, Joshua, had come to Austin for Thanksgiving. Matt was born and raised in San Antonio. After high school, he attended Blinn Community College for a year before transferring into Texas

A&M (yes, friends, he's an Aggie). He studied biology and agricultural engineering and recently started a job in civil engineering.

Matt is excited about his new job because the company is in the process of setting up a branch; and being on the ground floor, he gets the opportunity to gain valuable experience and help them grow. Matt is also focused on preventing flooding in Houston, where he now resides. As someone who went to help clean out houses flooded during hurricane Harvey, Matt said, "The pain that the residents go through seeing all of their treasures destroyed broke my heart." He feels it is his job as a civil engineer to help reduce those impacts and thinks the detaining of water on-site to slow the release of rainwater should, in turn, reduce the effects downstream.

Matt enjoys competing in obstacle course races and has sponsors. He recently returned from a two-week trip to Europe where he competed in the OCR Championships in London! While there, Matt also got the chance to visit Munich, Germany; Lauterbrunnen, Switzerland; and Amsterdam, Netherlands. Though it was a beautiful experience, Matt said he was glad to get back to Texas. He liked experiencing different cultures, but what he likes about Texas is the conservative culture and the sense of community where people help each other. The trip was a little challenging with the language barrier and not knowing how to read the signs when he was driving. I know the feeling. Please, meet Matt.

3

THE TOASTMASTERS INTERNATIONAL CONNECTION

"Ours is the only organization I know dedicated to the individual.
We work together to bring out the best in each of us,
and then we apply these skills to help others."

—Ralph Smedley, Founder of Toastmasters

Joining Toastmasters is one of the best decisions I've ever made. Let me say that again: joining Toastmasters is one of the best decisions I've ever made. I'm not going to apologize. It bears repeating. It is a non-profit, educational organization that teaches public speaking and leadership skills through a worldwide network of clubs.

The thought of speaking in front of even a small assembly of people used to terrify me, and now I am a professional public speaker. I learned so much more from Toastmasters than just speaking in front of a group. You can learn how to run a productive one-hour meeting, how to give constructive feedback, how to listen well, how to make others feel welcome, how to make room for a difference of opinion, and how to speak about controversial topics. It is a leadership laboratory. The advantages of being a Toastmaster go well beyond my lengthy list.

What I didn't expect when I joined Toastmasters was the lasting relationships I would form. I found that members of our club will come out to support me in other things I am doing. I make an effort to encourage them, also: not because I am returning a favor but because I genuinely want to. That's what friends do for one another—encourage and support. One of my friends from our club even gave me valuable advice and encouragement in writing this book. The friendships I have made over the years have been fantastic.

Initially, my husband lightheartedly described our local chapter as a glee club because we frequently clap for and encourage one another; most of the meetings he participated in as a military leader did not include such fervent and deliberate encouragement. He now gives the organization high marks as he has had a front-row seat to see just how supportive we are of each other and the benefits of that support.

I am continually telling job seekers, in my seminars and otherwise, of the many advantages of joining Toastmasters. One of the most valuable reasons to join is the networking aspect. Think about who would seek out a Toastmasters club: people who will be up in front of people speaking, like leaders of organizations who probably have influence in hiring practices and community leaders who know other community leaders, which can open doors. There is also the opportunity to network with members of other clubs, and then there are the Toastmaster holiday or year-end parties where you also get to mingle and get to know Toastmaster spouses or guests.

It just makes sense to me for a job seeker to search out these types of opportunities, but let us not limit the benefits to the job seeker. People do business with people they know, like, and trust. On a variety of occasions, I have observed people in our club doing business together because they like each other. Then, the more involved you are, the more likely you are to meet people in different clubs and get to know them. The people you will meet in this chapter, I met in some way, shape, or form through Toastmasters during my 100-day journey.

I will also say, there were others I met there who did not get included because I couldn't get around to everyone who came through our doors. As you will be able to glean from this first story, Toastmasters was a place I could count on to meet someone new during my challenge.

One late afternoon, as evening approached, I was fully aware of the fact that I had not met anyone new all day. Fortunately for me, it was a Toastmasters night. When I met Pam, she fulfilled my expectation to meet someone new. Pam is originally from Tennessee near Knoxville, but her family moved to Texas when she was in high school because her dad took a job at Texas Instruments. Pam's husband is from Houston, so she stayed in Texas while her brother hightailed it back to Tennessee as an adult. Pam also has two now-adult children. (Isn't it funny we don't have a word for our offspring who have grown up, like "adultren" or "childts?") Her daughter teaches school, and her son is studying for his doctorate in physical therapy.

Pam is a school administrator and has been asked to teach professional development around the state for the school system; hence, she came to check out our club. Now that she is an empty nester, Pam has set her sights on becoming a quality instructor and is looking to make new connections. Toastmasters can help expand her speaking toolset and make new friends. Please, meet Pam.

I met Christophe at Toastmasters. I did not get a chance to meet him when he came to his first meeting, so I made a point of introducing myself to him when I saw him at a later meeting. Christophe is from Belgium and moved to the U.S. for work in 1999. He started out in civil engineering but switched gears and moved to hospitality. That's a significant shift, but Christophe proves it is possible to change career paths. After retiring from hospitality, he now runs a few different businesses. One of his enterprises is Little Cyclist which offers balance bike training (a replacement for tricycles and training wheels) to children aged two years to five years. You can learn more about them at little-cyclist.com/home.

Christophe showed me a wedding picture with his wife and two sons, ages five and two-and-a-half. What was neat about this picture is that he was fulfilling a promise he made to his wife to marry her again every ten years; he had even written new vows for that occasion. For the married men out there, you might not want to let your wife read this.

Christophe has mentored young people and also worked alongside Child Protective Services (CPS) as a member of the Austin 20—a group of local individuals supporting organizations that find, protect, and restore survivors of domestic minor sex trafficking. He further explained they are trying to create a shelter for those needing a safe place to live. It is clear from talking to him that he has a real passion for making a difference in the world.

I am sure Christophe will have some exciting stories to tell about his life both before and after calling America his home. Please, meet Christophe.

Our guest speaker, one night at Toastmasters, was Cindy. She presented our chapter with an opportunity to help her high school seniors prepare for their future careers. During our chat after the meeting, I discovered she is the business teacher at our local high school who runs the internship and Senior Portfolio program. Her goal is to host a speaking series aimed at developing senior students' soft skills and covering important topics related to the job search after college.

The Senior Portfolio program is a requirement to graduate and is extremely valuable from a parent's perspective; it is an opportunity for the students to reflect on their time in high school and what they have learned. Each senior gives a presentation about their portfolio to a panel of guests. The collection includes the student's business resume, an activity resume, school transcript, letters of recommendation, college acceptance letters, awards, cover letters, and any other relevant documents. More importantly, putting their portfolio together is also a time for students to start planning for their future.

Cindy is originally from Austin, but she has also lived in Santé Fe, Kansas City, and San Antonio. She went to college at Texas Tech, where she met her husband and earned her MBA. Cindy has two children: a daughter working on her doctorate and a son working on his undergraduate degree. She said she took time off of work to raise her children but later went back to work because she wanted to do something for herself again. She taught community college for a while and felt good about herself at the end of the day.

Cindy took a job at the high school and became passionate about growing the business program there. She loves her job. She can get to know the students as people and help them make connections with the community by pairing them with mentors. Cindy gets joy out of facilitating those connections.

In her spare time, she likes to play tennis, water ski, and snow ski. She loves to read about business CEOs and historical fiction. We could have talked all night about historical fiction, as I am a fan too. As it turned out, we did talk until they closed the building. Please, meet Cindy.

Diana lives in my neighborhood. I have walked or driven past her home hundreds of times, yet I had never met her until she came to my Toastmasters club meeting, and I'm so glad she did. Diana grew up in a little town outside of San Antonio, Texas called Somerset and comes from a large family. She has seven siblings, and both of her parents each have seven siblings. That makes for huge family gatherings like her parent's recent fiftieth-anniversary celebration.

Diana told me she had a great childhood. Since she lived in a small town, everyone could participate in what they wanted, and she was quite involved: she played volleyball and basketball, ran track, was a cheerleader, and played in the band. In the group, she wanted to play the trumpet, but she ended up playing the family-owned clarinet instead. Diana is also fluent in Spanish. One story she shared with me about her childhood is that her mother had worked for AT&T as a phone operator. This was back in the days (not too long ago, mind you) when there was only one local phone company, and they had real humans operating the lines. When Diana called the operator one day, she got her mom and thought that was pretty cool.

Diana attended the University of Texas where she earned her bachelor's degree in nursing. The thing that stuck out the most to her after moving to Austin was how cold it was. That is because she grew up without air conditioning, and everywhere she went in Austin, the air conditioning was running. Of course, like most of us, she wouldn't dream of living without AC now. How quickly we adapt!

Diana has always been a high achiever, and school came easily to her. She started her professional career as an operating-room nurse. What struck me in our conversation was her passion for patient care. It wasn't long before people were telling her she should become a doctor. Instead of going back to school, she pursued a management position and was very successful. She started working in marketing, then with mergers and acquisitions. Before she knew it, Diana had become the CEO of a small surgical hospital at twenty-eight years old. She eventually went back to school for her MBA.

Diana is married and is a mother. After working long hours and traveling extensively, she decided to step away for a while. Family is vital to her, and she wanted to put more of her attention there. It also gave her time to work on a couple of her other passions—design is one of them. She designed and produced a healthcare analytics software program, which will allow the hospitals to provide better care, in addition to teaching herself Auto CAD, a design and drafting software. She and a partner built the healthcare analytics software and sold it to a global software company. As for the Auto CAD, well, she designed and built her parents a home; thus began her successful remodeling and home construction business.

Now Diana wants to turn her attention to giving back to her community in a different way. She had been asked to be the guest speaker on several occasions and is contemplating doing more public speaking to inspire others. She said, "We all have a story to tell and audiences that should hear it." I would have to agree with her. Because of her passion for patient care, she is open to other possibilities in this arena. Please, meet Diana.

My friend and fellow Toastmaster, Nicole, introduced me to her husband, Travis, at a party Joel and I attended. He is a lawyer by trade and graciously agreed to meet and tell me his story. A native of Texas, Travis was born in Austin and raised on a ranch in Dripping Springs. He has three older half-brothers, an older half-sister, a younger sister, and a younger brother. I asked Travis if he had always wanted to be a lawyer, and he told me an interesting story. It turns out he was not interested in the law when he left high school.

Travis had been accepted to Stanford, which was his dream school. However, due to a misunderstanding, he chose to go in-state. You see, when he received his acceptance letter, he told his mother, who was very excited for him, but when they broke the news to his father, he said, "Well, sure you can go to Stanford, but I will only pay for Texas." His dad was kidding, of course, but at seventeen, Travis did not understand sarcasm and took his father's words literally. Imagine his father's dismay when he found out his son was going to Texas Tech instead of Stanford because of his jesting! By the time Travis realized his father had been joking, he had missed the deadline for the down payment to Stanford, and off to Texas Tech he went.

Lubbock was so unlike what he was used to that he returned home seven months later. Not knowing what to do next, he went to work at a law firm based on a friend's recommendation. That job turned him totally off to the law profession, and he went back to school. This time he tried the University of Texas, which is where his father had gone to school. He took a winding path and ended back at Texas Tech. This time he graduated. It was during his second stint at Texas Tech that he was inspired to study the law.

During his time there, the Texas Tech president censored student organizations. Travis thought this was in breach of one of his values: the First Amendment. When Travis found out he was entirely wrong on the point and it wasn't a breach, he decided to go to law school and study constitutional law. Thinking he wanted to become a law professor, he even got a second degree in comparative constitutional law. Then reality hit; he learned this field paid very little, so he switched gears to practice litigation instead.

Travis discovered he loves litigation—not so much the prep work, but he enjoys the actual courtroom stuff. He said it's like a game. You keep score, and you find out at the end if you put the puzzle pieces together in a way to make a compelling case to others who know nothing about the situation. Do they see the puzzle the same way? Can you win them over?

Travis is a capable person and is passionate about working with his hands. He enjoys art photography, oil painting, woodworking, fly fishing (he ties his own flies, by the way), and building workshops and storage sheds. He also designs the blueprints and creates the materials lists for the structures he builds.

Two men greatly influenced Travis: his father and grandfather. Both were self-sufficient men. He learned carpentry from his grandfather. When he worked with his father side-by-side to build his grandparents a house on his father's ranch, he gained even more knowledge. They also taught him mechanical things. He hopes to pass this knowledge on to his two sons who are currently ages six and four.

Travis is proud of his heritage and rightly so. His father was a sophomore on a baseball scholarship at the University of Texas when Japan bombed Pearl Harbor. His dad withdrew from all of his classes the following day and joined the war effort. The Army Air Corps trained him to become a fighter pilot. In those days, the Army issued each person a shotgun to practice shooting clay pigeons to help them become accurate shooters. At the end of that war, his dad was able to buy that shotgun for fifty cents, which he later gave to Travis. All told, his father served in WWII, Vietnam, and Korea; he traveled all over Europe, the Middle East, Northern Africa, and the Pacific before retiring.

During our conversation, Travis told me about a time when he was twenty-five, and his father took him to Africa. One day he was sitting by a watering hole waiting to see the animals that would come for a drink. He got separated from his father and the only other person in their party (already something doesn't sound quite right about where this is going). Travis had been waiting a while and was getting bored, so he was playing around with his 35mm Minolta camera. Then, he heard some rustling coming from the grassy area nearby. The tall grass parted and out of it came a gigantic head attached to the body of a lion! It was a lioness, not fifteen feet from where he was. There she stood, looking right at him. He was so startled that he accidentally hit the shutter release on his camera and took a picture of her. The noise so alarmed the lioness that she bounded away. I want to see that picture! Please, meet Travis.

I met Melinda at a party. She is married to Jay, a friend of mine through Toastmasters. Melinda was born in Houston but grew up in New Orleans. She and Jay met when he was a teacher's assistant. He was teaching the only class that would fit her schedule one summer, and she needed that credit to graduate. They married a couple of years later. After completing her undergraduate degree, Melinda got a master's degree in audiology.

Melinda taught audiology to graduate students and first-year medical students at Louisiana State University School of Medicine. She did that until she and Jay moved to Austin. Once in Austin, Melinda thought she would pursue her doctorate. Unfortunately, she arrived mid-semester and would need to wait six months for the next semester to start, so Melinda went to work with a friend of theirs in real estate instead. She did quite well and sold the very first house she ever showed. After working in the field for six years, she decided to try her hand in commercial real estate before eventually branching off into feasibility studies and analysis (for developments and subdivisions). With each job, she found herself working for a different firm. By then she was the mother of twin girls.

Things were going along smoothly until the bottom fell out of the real estate market in Austin, and the city of Austin instituted a busing policy. Melinda was not comfortable with the idea her children would have to get up extra early and travel a long distance to school when there was a perfectly good school close by. These two separate and unrelated events led to their decision to make a big change.

Jay and Melinda decided to pick up and move to Ashville, Tennessee. It was a gutsy move because they went to Ashville without either of them having a job, and their house was under contract but not sold. One thing that must have been a shock to them was that when they left Austin, it was May and ninety-seven degrees outside. When they arrived in Ashville a couple of days later, there was frost on the ground, and the heater in the home they had just purchased wouldn't work. That's a moment when you say, "Aye, aye, aye!" They started to second-guess their decision but ended up staying for seven years and loved it.

In Ashville, Melinda shifted her career to freelance advertising, public relations, and writing. This experience helped her realize audiology was not her passion; her passion was art. She had been pursuing art until her college advisor intervened, after her third semester, and steered her away from it. Her advisor acknowledged her passion for art but candidly suggested she look around at the competition. By the way, I saw some of her artwork, and I think it's beautiful. She has other admirers too, as she has sold some of her work. I will show you one of her pieces below. Instead of art, Melinda went after her second love—writing. She had minored in both sociology and English.

Melinda, Jay, and their girls moved back to Austin to be closer to the family after Melinda's father became ill. It was easier to get to her mom and brother who live in New Orleans and her sister, who lives in Dallas.

Speaking of family, I asked Melinda what it was like to be the mother of twins. She said the first six months were awful because the girls were on different schedules; but once the routine was ironed out, she declared it a terrific experience. Her twins were best friends, and they still are today. She and Jay have a great relationship with their girls and are now thrilled to be the grandparents of a three, two, and one year old. Melinda shared that when they all get together, "It's crazy but fun!"

In Austin, Melinda was still doing freelance writing but was looking for something else when she came across Dr. Buchanan, who practices family medicine. He knew that fourteen years ago she and Jay had started a wellness company working with different hospitals around the country. So he asked her if she would be interested in running the wellness clinic he was getting ready to open. Perfect timing, perfect fit.

Melinda is multi-talented and has several hobbies. She likes working in her vegetable garden and her yard. She enjoys horseback riding on her horse on occasion; she would do it more often, but the beautiful horse is getting old, and arthritis is setting in. She makes beautiful art, and she still enjoys writing. She has published two children's books, a cookbook, and a novel. Her books are highly rated; at the writing of this book, her cookbook is rated five stars, and her novel has four and a half stars. You can find them on Amazon by doing an author search: Melinda West Seifert. Please, meet Melinda.

I met Marguerite at a Toastmasters meeting; she happened to be sitting right beside me. I found out she recently moved to the area from California but is originally from Memphis, Tennessee.

Marguerite is married and comes from a large family by today's standards, being one of six kids. It is amazing to me who I meet and what I learn when I initiate a conversation with someone.

Early in her career, Marguerite worked on the movie Great Balls of Fire in the late eighties when they were filming in Memphis. At the end of that project, connections she made told her to come to Los Angeles, and "they" would get her work. Marguerite made the move, and she was in the movie business for a while as the art department coordinator and later moved to production.

"It was a crazy business," she said, and also fun and full of lessons. Marguerite worked and interacted with a few people, perhaps you have heard of some of them: Dennis Quaid, Clint Eastwood, and Tom Hanks. I couldn't resist, I had to ask her what it was like working with big named stars in Hollywood. Not surprisingly, they're all individuals—just like anybody else. She did say Tom Hanks is a sweetheart.

Marguerite moved to Northern California to be close to her sister, which is also where she met her husband. When they got married, her husband's job transferred them to Southern California, and they lived there for fifteen years. During that time, Marguerite owned a business where she specialized in helping people get over addictions, severe trauma, child abuse, divorce—anything emotional. She is trained in the techniques of Tapping, neuro-linguistic programming (NLP), and hypnotherapy. All three modalities help people break through subconscious beliefs that control their behaviors and outcomes. She has worked with people both in and out of treatment centers.

I found it interesting to learn that Marguerite worked with a long-term addiction treatment facility in Hawaii, where the residents stayed for three years. For her part, she would live with them for two weeks and do sessions all day long. Marguerite helped the residents deal with their childhood traumas, which most—if not all of them—had. She was very excited about this work because of the drastic changes she could see in those with whom she worked.

Moving from California to Austin, Marguerite is retiring from her trauma work and is now reinventing herself in real estate. While she will help people from time to time with trauma, she said after ten years, it is time for a change. That type of work can be draining, and she is ready to engage with people on a different level. When people are buying a home, they are generally happy about it. She feels she is still helping people achieve a level of happiness while they make one of the most significant purchases of their lives.

Marguerite loves to write. She authored the book *Let It Go*, which is available for purchase on Amazon. In addition to writing, she enjoys Toastmasters and has the goal of competing in the world championships and winning. She says, "Why not swing for the fences? If you have a big goal like that, even if you land short of it, you've really grown."

Marguerite fairly quickly joined our Toastmasters group. We have met several times outside of these meetings, and she even provided some wise counsel regarding the writing of this book. I count her as a friend. Please, meet Marguerite.

Terry visited our Toastmaster's club after I started my challenge. He decided to join us and has been coming for several weeks, yet I had not had the opportunity to meet him other than to say hello. I finally approached him to get better acquainted. As we sat and talked over coffee, I discovered he is an accomplished person who has a very positive outlook despite a less than ideal childhood and young adult life.

Terry was born in Odessa but later moved with his family to Ft. Stockton, Texas. His parents divorced when he was in third grade, and life became very complicated. He and his mother moved to Ruidoso, Texas. Terry has a sister who is ten years older than he is, so she was out of the home by that time. At eight years old, he assumed the role of the man of the house and took on a lot of responsibility for the home while his mom worked a lot. His dad was still active in his life, and Terry would spend the summers with him until his dad became very ill. Terry was eleven when he lost his father to cancer. During his father's illness, many unfortunate and complex extended family dynamics developed. Terry and his mom moved again, as she was pursuing career training, but the public-school system where they moved proved to be less than desired. The decision was made for Terry to move to a better school district—without his mom; he was only around fifteen or sixteen. He lived with a family friend, who himself was only twenty-five. The truth is Terry was responsible for himself at a very young age. In his junior year, his mother was diagnosed with stage four lymphoma. Thankfully, she defied the odds. Twenty years later, she is doing reasonably well.

Terry has been blessed with a great intellect. After taking the PSAT, he was offered a partial scholarship to Yale; he was still not able to attend. Terry looks back on that and says, "Everything happens for a reason." He started at a junior college instead. Much of the time, he was working in healthcare and going to school. There were times he would have to put school on pause to work, then put work on pause to go back to school; he was determined to finish. It took him eight years to work his way through college. During that time, he was consistently available to his mom as she was undergoing chemotherapy treatments. Terry graduated from Tarleton State University with an undergraduate degree in international business and went on to earn his MBA from the University of Phoenix. He embodies the phrase "where there is a will there is a way."

Terry moved to Austin, exactly where he wanted to be, and continued to work in healthcare. Once he had his degrees, he progressed up the corporate ladder. Terry has an entrepreneurial spirit. He developed software to help decrease healthcare supply costs, which he was able to present to the government in Puerto Rico right before its financial collapse. Terry joined a corporate Toastmasters club to improve his presentation skills for work and held various leadership roles in that club. He joined the Dripping Springs club—a community club—which he said has a different feel to it. Terry has also challenged himself by taking on home remodeling projects instead of hiring them out. That is not surprising as he has been very self-reliant for much of his life.

Terry told me his outlook on life is that if there are roadblocks along the way, they are there for a reason. If an obstacle comes up, that means he's supposed to be doing something different. "There is a plan for everybody, and that plan isn't a straight line. Free will is there, and we exercise it; then, we're directed back to where we need to be."

He enjoys traveling and has visited China, the United Kingdom, Costa Rica, and Panama. He's played rugby and has backpacked thru rainforests. Before we ended our conversation, Terry shared something I thought was very profound—he said that when he meets people, he tries to experience them from their story versus putting them up against his. In other words, instead of passing judgment, he tries to see their point of view. Very cool. Please, meet Terry.

4

SERENDIPITY

"People come into your life for a reason, a season, or a lifetime."

—Author Unknown

There have been countless times when a stranger has entered my life by a chance meeting; I like to think of them as divine appointments. Do you ever evaluate those chance meetings? Did they impact you in some way? Maybe it was you who influenced them, and you may never know precisely how. Sometimes, it is once many years have gone by that you look back and see how one chance meeting had a dramatic effect on your life. Perhaps that person became a trusted friend, an advocate, or a mentor. And of course, we have often heard of chance meetings leading to romance, but we'll save that for another chapter. The point is, at the time you meet someone, you can't immediately tell the value of the relationship that will develop or how your chance meeting will later impact your life. It is only with time and reflection that you begin to glean its worth. Let me tell you of one such occurrence in my youth.

It was my senior year at the Air Force Academy. It was nearing the time to select a career field for those of us who were not going to be pilots. A friend of mine, Michele, and I started talking about the contracting career field as a possible choice. It sounded interesting, but I didn't know much about contract work. I made a call to the contracting office located at the academy to see if there was someone I could talk to who was already involved with it as a profession. I wanted to know if I could have a conversation with somebody to become more knowledgeable on the subject. The way you got into that career field at the time was to go before a selection board. You had to be interviewed for it since it was a competitively selected position. I was lucky; a lieutenant colonel, which was a high-ranking officer to any cadet, agreed to meet with me. I asked him every question I knew to ask and thanked him for his time. When the board finally met several weeks later, I walked in, and to my surprise, that very same lieutenant colonel was one of three members on the selection board. Needless to say, I was chosen to enter that career field; I call that serendipity.

That was my first encounter with an informational interview, and it led immediately to a career opportunity, which is something I teach to my job seekers today. Those types of interviews are instrumental in finding out about opportunities, as well as gaining access to knowledge invaluable in the job hunt.

One day, I went for a walk with my friend Tina. As we were approaching a house, Leah waved at us and called out to Tina. You see, Leah and Tina are friends—not surprising, as Tina knows just about everybody; I am fortunate to call her my friend.

Leah wanted to show Tina her backyard remodel project-in-progress. Naturally, I got to tag along. Leah's yard is going to be gorgeous. There is one area where the terrain was very steep. I wouldn't have known what to do with it, but her remodel was far enough along for me to see her vision coming together. I even got a few ideas for an area in my backyard. The pictures were taken towards the top of the incline. Leah is remarkably talented.

After Tina made the appropriate introductions, I explained my 100-day project to Leah, who was fascinated by the idea. She agreed to participate and is also considering doing a challenge herself. Let me tell you about her.

Leah owns Better Bites Bakery, which started in Dripping Springs just a couple of years ago. Better Bites Bakery is a gluten-free, kosher, non-GMO, top eight allergen-free bakery. The store was created out of necessity because her youngest son was diagnosed with anaphylactic allergies. There is absolutely a market for her products. I was in her bakery shortly after we moved to Dripping Springs when I was looking for bread made without yeast, but that's a tough one, and they didn't have those.

Leah outgrew her first location and has recently moved her operations to Dallas. Her products can be found in a lot of stores like Albertsons, HEB, Central Market, Whole Foods, and a host of others in Texas. You can read about her journey on her website, and while you're there, check out her goodies too! http://www.betterbitesbakery.com/our-story.

(Second picture of yard was taken one year later.)

There are a lot of new people moving to Dripping Springs. Dorothy and her husband recently moved here from Houston. She also has a sister who moved here ten years ago. I would like to complain about the massive influx of people into Dripping Springs and how it is changing our town (notice how quickly I take ownership and say "our"), but I've only been here for four years.

It's confession time. I have walked right by Dorothy at least three or four times, never stopping for a conversation. I just gave her a smile, a wave, and mouthed a brief, "Hi." We both frequent the same spot, and she always smiled back. I didn't know Dorothy was new to Dripping Springs. So what made this day any different? I'd decided to be intentional about connecting with others—that's it. It was to my benefit to meet another friendly person.

Dorothy retired from the oil and gas banking industry, which is different from the oil and gas industry. Her job was to finance the folks in the oil and gas industry. I had never really thought of banking as being specialized by trade area, but it makes sense. I knew there were mortgage loan officers and investment bankers, but I had just never thought of it as an industry with segregated specialties. She has enjoyed meeting many people through her church, volunteering, and working on a political campaign. Please, meet Dorothy.

Working from home does have its challenges for an extrovert like me, so I occasionally go to other places to work or conduct meetings. I met Kendal at Starbucks. We were both sitting at a communal table waiting on our respective two o'clock appointments. I thought her glasses were pretty cool.

As we exchanged pleasantries, we unanimously agreed that the room temperature was a little too cold for our liking. Our consensus about the room temperature started our conversation. I learned Kendal had recently moved back to the Austin area with her husband and four children. I also learned she is an advocate for foster children and recruits people to become foster parents.

Kendal shared with me some facts on the overwhelming need in our country for foster parents and explained the challenge of recruiting couples. It is a big 'ask' to request someone to love on a child or children knowing it is only for a season. As we discussed the topic of fostering children, Kendal helped me reshape my perspective and focus from the impact these temporary arrangements have on foster parents to the reflective lens of the child. Even for a season, a foster parent can dramatically and positively impact that child for a lifetime.

If you have ever thought about becoming a foster parent—or want more information on other ways you can make a positive impact in a foster child's life—reach out to the Arrow Organization at www.arrow.org. Please, meet Kendal.

I unexpectedly met Don at a block party. Don is the father of James, who is one of our neighbors. Don is a former military pilot and currently lives in Florida. He is retired, but he grows apples, pears, and cherries. He also owns a few commercial buildings and pipe laying equipment, and he developed a gated community too. Doesn't sound like retirement to me—I'm just sayin'. Don also has a philanthropic side as he has done quite a bit of charitable work in Africa.

Don caught me off guard because he brought up politics at the party during our initial conversation; I mean, we had not even been properly introduced. We came from very different perspectives, but we gave each other the courtesy of listening to each other's thoughts. We must have talked for at least an hour. In the end, I listened to a symposium he recommended and learned quite a bit. I sent him some information, and I hope he will take the time to read through it with an open mind.

Often, when I take the time to share my perspective and listen with an open mind to someone else, at the very least, there is a mutual understanding of our varying points of view. Sometimes we have to agree to disagree, and that's okay too.

Don is a grandfather and a very confident, competent businessman who is enjoying his life and his family. His grandchildren were enjoying him too; they threw him a ball which landed twice in his plate. He calmly picked it up, the ball a little worse for wear, and threw it back to them each time. By the time we were able to take our photo together, it was getting quite late. Please, meet Don.

I met Dede when I went out to lunch to celebrate a mutual friend's birthday. Dede is the mother of six grown children. As a military dependent, she moved quite a bit and has lived in eleven states and two foreign countries—Germany and Spain.

Dede spends time traveling and visiting her children, as they are quite spread out—two are in Alaska, two travel with the military, one is in Dubai, and one lives in Austin. She recently took a road trip with her twenty-nine year-old son. The birthday group was impressed that her son had invited his mom to travel with him. We were also impressed that Dede was willing to be so flexible since the trip was much unplanned as far as the travel details went. For instance, they did not have hotels pre-booked. It was a mother's love, or perhaps she is just as adventurous as her son.

It turns out that Dede and I have a lot in common. She homeschooled her children like I did (except I only taught two while she taught six), and we have both been to Kadena Air Base in Okinawa, Japan. We have also both experienced and miss the camaraderie that comes with the military way of life.

Dede enjoys spending time with her grandchildren and being in community with other women. We talked about a lot of things like the difference in the expectations of life among different generations and Tricare (military healthcare) of all things. Her experience with the military was from the Army side while mine was the Air Force. Dede led a group of women in the study of a book called *Sit, Walk, Stand* by Watchman Nee; I joined her in that study, so we had the opportunity to spend quality time together and get to know each other. Please, meet Dede.

I had the opportunity to meet Elizabeth and Clotilde at a coffee house called Mazama Coffee Co. My friend, Jackie and I found ourselves in a discussion about one of the topics I speak and teach on: networking. She asked me if I would meet with her and Elizabeth, and I was happy to do so. Elizabeth happened to bring her eighty-one-year-young mother, Clotilde, along.

Jackie and Elizabeth are neighbors and are preparing to go into real estate together. Elizabeth is married and has a daughter, Sophie. Elizabeth and her family have a passion for horses; they currently have a horse and a pony and are looking for an addition.

Elizabeth stages houses for realtors and Clotilde had driven up from San Antonio to help her with staging a home in the Dripping Springs area. I love to see strong mother-daughter relationships. Elizabeth's family has been in the real estate business for a long time, and that is how she learned to stage properties for sale.

She loves to design and has mastered the process of creating new spaces. Her eyes light up when she talks about it. You can find her design and staging work on her website at www.plethoradecor.com. Now she is ready to sell homes and has a vision of offering her staging skills as part of her real estate services.

Clotilde has a quiet spirit, but don't let that fool you! She has led quite a fascinating life! She has traveled all over Europe and has made two trips to Jerusalem. She said she got a chance to walk where Jesus walked and feels very blessed to have done so: and she wants to go back. Clotilde has also been to Hawaii. She and I talked about how blue the water is there and that once you've been to Hawaii, you get spoiled by its beauty. She challenged me to take a cruise. I told her that they sound lovely except for one thing—you are surrounded by water. I mentioned I wouldn't mind taking a river cruise where I could still see land. Elizabeth piped back in and asked me in which branch of the service I had served. She said, "Surely, not the navy!" Ha! She was right. Please, meet Elizabeth and Clotilde.

I had the good fortune to have coffee with two very accomplished women: Dana and Katja. I met them at a fireside chat I was co-leading on the subject of having difficult conversations. I will introduce you to Dana first and Katja in the next story. It turns out they are both fellow coaches, so natural curiosity and spirit of friendship developed among the three of us.

Dana is from San Diego, California. She got dual degrees in communications and sociology from the University of California, Santa Barbara and played a lot of Frisbee golf. Like most young people who are not sure exactly what they want to do, Dana learned by trial-and-error what she didn't want to do. She started her career in social work, then worked as an instructional aide, and later as a florist. Although she rose to management quickly in floral design, she learned that working with flowers can be dangerous business. Her third set of stitches convinced her to change career fields once more. She still likes to arrange bouquets, but only for fun now.

Dana has fourteen-year-old twin boys whom she's raised the last several years as a single parent. She said they function well together as a team and their future is very bright. Life is filled with twists and turns, and you never know what joys lay around the corner. Dana is fun and full of laughter. I loved hearing her laugh as she told her story. Her quest for learning compelled her to go back to school for broadcasting; she learned broadcast journalism, media production, and editing. Dana even put on a show in New York, including being up on stage. She later worked for an independently owned TV station where she got the opportunity to produce mini-documentaries. In the end, she discovered the high-stress environment was not her cup of tea.

Still searching for her passion, Dana met a coach named Tonya, and her world opened up. She said she learned a lot of things about herself working with Tonya and evolved as a person. That pushed her into the world of coaching; she has been a coach for the past sixteen years and thoroughly enjoys it. Dana was trained in the Sage Method, which allowed her to follow her coaching passions—family systems, creating businesses with joy and purpose, and highlighting, evaluating and researching human development systems. Check out her website at www.danasmycoach.com. I love the questions she asks her clients, for example, "How would you be different if you dared to dream?"

Dana recently went back to school again, this time to earn a master's degree in program evaluation and administration, specializing in family and child development. She is also an author and has written two books. She dubs herself a reformed achiever and reformed cat lover; only time will tell. I see accomplishment after accomplishment. And I didn't know it was possible to, at one time, love cats and then not, but okay, I'll buy the reformation there. I also discovered Dana loves the color pink. She wears it well. Please, meet Dana.

I mentioned that I met Katja (pronounced Kät-ti-a) when I met Dana. Katja is from West Berlin, Germany, and grew up quite close to the Berlin Wall. To her, it was not a big deal; she thought it was normal and that every city had a wall around it with checkpoints.

She is the only child of two artists. One was a dancer and the other a musician. They worked for the government and traveled the world performing. As a result, she too loved to travel and recalls her childhood as being fun. Whenever her parents had a summer vacation, which for Germans was typically six weeks a year, or even just a day off, her family would travel—mostly up and down Italy. To her, travel was as ordinary as brushing your teeth. She was shocked when she met people in Berlin that had never even left their neighborhood.

Given her background, it was only natural that she jumped at the chance to do an exchange program and came to America at sixteen. When she returned to Germany, Katja thought she wanted to be a psychotherapist for kids but realized she didn't have the grades to qualify for that. Instead, she did a three-year internship program. After her internship, she decided she needed to learn French, so she moved to France.

When the wall came down, Katja was finally able to go to a university in East Germany to study for her master's degree in psychology. University in Germany at that time was free. She did not tell her classmates she was from West Germany because they would not have treated her the same. It was a turbulent time, and East Germans felt it was a takeover by West Germany. In the end, it was. East German companies were taken over by West Germans.

During her University time, Katja traveled to Austria, Czechia, Hungary, Switzerland, and then back to America for another exchange program. This time, she landed at City College in Harlem, and it was exciting. That is where she met her husband, who was also an exchange student but from Munich. Though he is German, he lived in Mexico until he was nine years old.

After she got her degree in industrial psychology, Katja went to work doing consumer research for Mercedes. She worked with a great team, but the meaning in her work was missing. While working there, she got married and started a family. Katja decided to leave her full-time job and eventually discovered coaching; she realized she could enjoy her work and get paid for it. She met a coach, Martin, who also coached Dana (from the previous story); that is what brought the two of them together.

Katja, her husband, and two sons eventually left Germany. They lived in Brazil, for six months, returned to live in Germany for three years, and then lived in Switzerland for four years before moving to America, where they currently reside. They have been here now for one year. Katja is a high-performance coach and still travels regularly back to Germany for work. Visit her website at www.katjarossel.info. Please, meet Katja.

I went to a training on entrepreneur business coaching held by . . . did you guess Dana and Katja? If you did, you would be correct; it was a great session, by the way. At the meeting, I happened to meet Lissie, whose passion and business is centered on creating joy. Lissie came into the room, and the atmosphere changed. She is bright and upbeat; when I say bright, I mean that literally. She wore a shimmering silver jacket and had on a bedazzled top with sparkly earrings, but she wasn't overdone.

Lissie was born in the Dallas area and moved around Texas quite a bit growing up. She is an Aggie. If you know anything about Texas schools, then you know a lot about her already based on that tidbit of information. She was very interested in English as a major; her mother, who was paying the bill, did not approve. She switched from a degree in English to psychology but then entered the field of broadcasting. As a student, she worked part-time at the school radio station. Once she graduated, she was offered a full-time position.

Lissie has done a variety of jobs in broadcasting and other fields; some of the roles she had were in production, in hosting shows, and in directing the programs. One of the jobs she is most proud of is when she lived in San Antonio, TX. While there, she helped underprivileged high school graduates research their career opportunities and go to trade schools. Lissie lived in several other places before finally moving back to Austin, TX to settle down with her husband, Jim, of twenty-three years. They have one daughter who lights up their life.

Professionally, Lissie eventually obtained her masters in English. It came in handy when she sought and was hired for a position as a high school English teacher. While Lissie loves English, she did not like teaching it. Lately, Lissie has been doing what she calls her "side hustles," which she thoroughly enjoys. She makes costumes for ballet performances and children who wish to dress up as characters from their favorite books. She writes songs and teaches voice lessons; Lissie believes that if you can talk, you can sing. (Okay, she is giving me a measure of hope here). She sings in nursing homes and in particular likes working with patients who have Alzheimer's disease. With those patients, she will often sing old hymns. Even though Alzheimer patients don't remember a lot of things, they tend to liven up when they hear familiar tunes. Lissie says it is so delightful to see the joyful response of the family members when they catch a glimpse of their loved one singing, even if only for a short while.

She also speaks once a month at a church where she used to be the music director. A couple of the topics she speaks on are forgiving yourself and forgiving others. When she is not making costumes, teaching, or singing, you may find her writing. She has authored a book entitled *Energize Your Dreams Day by Day* and is getting ready to start on her new book. Did I mention she also has quite a few videos on YouTube? You can check out her website to get more information at www.lissienow.com.

In her "spare time," if you could call it that, Lissie enjoys traveling with her family and helps her husband in the office with his construction business. Please, meet Lissie.

I met Ashley when I was talking to our mutual friends, Lauren and John, and she happened to walk past. John mentioned my challenge to her. We exchanged numbers, and she agreed to meet later. Ashley is from the Texas panhandle, where her father was a corn grower. Her family moved to Waco, Texas, when she was in the second grade. Ashley is married and has two daughters, who are eleven and twelve. She also has an older brother.

After college, Ashley moved to Dallas to work for Morgan Stanley as a broker-in-training. While she was studying for her series six and seven exams (for investment licensing), she realized she did not like the work—even though she had studied business management and finance in school. While working at Morgan Stanley, she was recruited away to join the number one executive recruiting firm, Korn Ferry, International. I'm not sure if they were number one when she started working there, but they did receive that distinction in 2017. She was later recruited away from them by Spencer Stuart, which is another executive recruiting firm. She discovered that she loved being an executive recruiter.

Ashley's girls are eighteen months apart and are currently in the fifth and seventh grades. Her younger daughter loves horses and is involved in show jumping and dressage. Her older daughter has very different interests: she loves school, tennis, track, and volleyball. Ashley describes her as the family's social butterfly. In addition to keeping up with the girls' jumping, dressage, tennis, track, and volleyball activities, Ashley also homeschools her daughters two days a week and is enjoying being a mom.

I asked Ashley what she does for fun. Traveling and hiking with her family are right at the top of the list. She shared that her husband is a great cook and foodie. He is a first-generation American, and both of his parents came from Italy; they once took a trip to Italy and tried to eat their way across the country. How's that for a challenge? Ashley includes Pilates as part of her weekly routine because it centers her mind. She also loves to read and has read thirty-five books so far this year; she wishes books had a rating system like the movies have. Ashley gets disappointed when she picks up a book and starts to get into it only to find the language or content is not desirable. In addition to all of this other reading, she still sets aside time to read her Bible. During our conversation, we covered a myriad of topics, including politics, the NFL, and raising kids; I really enjoyed our visit. You can read her husband's story in Chapter 8. Please, meet Ashley.

Nearing the end of the year, I happened to be clear across town in Cedar Park when I spied an Office Depot, and I ran in quickly to take care of an errand. I needed to buy a calendar for the upcoming year. Whom do I run into? Terry, of course! Okay, so I didn't know Terry; he happened to come into the calendar aisle while I was deciding amongst my various options. He was being friendly and spoke first.

Terry: "Hi, how are you?"

Me: "Great, thank you. You have a very nice smile!"

A few minutes pass as he continues on his mission and I debate, should I? Should I not? I decided to go for it. "Hey, since you have such a nice smile, I have to ask you,..." Terry was so kind; he accepted my challenge. Our conversation was brief because Terry was making a quick stop during his workday, but he still took a few minutes to chat with me.

Terry was born in Indianapolis, but he considers Austin home. He has lived here for the last thirty-five years. He has two siblings: a brother and a sister. Terry is also married and has two children. After high school, he did electrician work, and he learned the old-fashioned way: on the job. Today he is the founding partner of a home and commercial security company called Dynamic Total Protection Services which can be found at dtpsaustin.com.

After being an electrician, Terry went to the low voltage side of it and started pulling wire and installing security systems. Then he had the thought, why do this work for other companies when I can start my own? He has been doing this work for the past twenty-two years.

In his free time, Terry likes to fish, hunt, and coach his daughters in fastpitch softball. When I asked him if he would like to share anything else, he said, "I have worked hard all my life to establish everything I've gotten today, and that's all because of the glory of God." Please, meet Terry.

5

RESILIENCE

"In every life we have some trouble
But when you worry you make it double
Don't worry, be happy"

—Bobby McFerrin

The human spirit is resilient. We were created that way because adversity is a fact of life. Resilience is about finding a way to rise above life's challenges. Some of us are more resilient than others. According to the article, "Resilience" in *Psychology Today*, resilience is a quality that can be cultivated. Some of the factors that make people more resilient are having a positive attitude, the ability to regulate their emotions, and the ability to see failure as a form of helpful feedback. Further, optimism helps blunt the impact of stress on the mind and body.

Each of the stories you are about to read includes some element of resilience. Most of them are work-related. Many people attach their identity to their work—though I wish that were not so—but in that light, when one's life's work changes, it can be a significant emotional event requiring grit to navigate. In my professional coaching, I regularly advise people to set up and follow a schedule when looking for work. By having a plan, you are strategizing and setting goals, which makes you forward-thinking and, by definition, a bit more optimistic. The same would hold true for an entrepreneur or the currently working employee if you think about that statement and follow the logic. Okay, that's my plug for goal setting.

There are stories of resilience through many stages of life—from just starting, to the middle of the road; then there is the closing of one chapter and beginning another. The more optimistically you approach each situation, the more likely you are to navigate the twists and turns well. Life's going to happen (unless it doesn't). My philosophy is, either way, being negative won't help.

I met an amazing young man named Stefan at a conference held at the Sententia Vera Cultural Hub in Dripping Springs. Stephan hails from East Lyme, Connecticut. He graduated from Quinnipiac University with a degree in interactive media. He is the oldest of four and has three brothers all very close in age. Stefan moved to Austin in 2017 while his youngest brother was attending the University of Texas. He is a videographer, editor, and GFX Designer.

Stefan began his career working in television news but found the environment did not fit his passions and interests. The constant focus on negative news affected him deeply, despite his interest in current events. When he started his career in television, the Ebola virus was in the global spotlight, and Robin Williams had recently passed away. Stefan found himself editing fifty elements of over fifty pieces of mainly negative video every day: it was a lot to absorb. This experience was in stark contrast to what he had experienced as an intern.

During his internship, Stefan was a photographer for the news' website's entertainment section. He covered concerts such as Roger Waters from Pink Floyd and sporting events. He was given fun assignments like capturing pup night at the Pittsburgh Pirate's stadium. He said, "I'm not a sports person, but sitting up in the broadcast booth way above home plate—that was pretty cool!" I mention his internship in detail because it was pivotal in the direction he has chosen to pursue.

Trying to figure out where he wanted to focus his future work, Stefan met with his high school video production teacher. This teacher—a mentor he had kept in touch with—asked him if he would be interested in videoing a wedding for a family friend. When Stefan said yes, his mentor recommended him, and Stefan got the job. The newlyweds loved his work, so his mentor provided additional referrals. Stefan learned he enjoyed this work. Now his motto is he loves "capturing life's positive moments," and that has become his life goal. He told me, "I want to cover events. I just want to be at the center of someone's happiness and someone's best moments. I want to capture that." Stefan remarked that it could be selling a home, a celebration, a concert, and of course a wedding—anything that brings people together in community.

Some of his hobbies include hiking, being a tourist in a new city, taking a road trip, or just plain exploring. Of course, he takes pictures and mini videos along the way. He took an exciting road trip along the coast of Florida and has set a goal of driving the whole Pacific Coast Highway one day. Stefan really enjoys observing. He said with video and journalism, "You have to be a good observer. You're not the story; often, you get one shot to get it right."

I enjoyed our conversation and learned a lot from Stefan. He was very authentic in our discussion about his experiences. I have been following him on Instagram and Facebook, and I have to say he does some fantastic work. He captures life's beautiful moments in such a way that I feel I am right there on the scene. If you need someone with his skills, check out more of his work on Instagram @AleoMedia. Stefan is usually behind the camera, but he let me take his picture for my 100 people in 100 days challenge. Please, meet Stefan.

I would like to introduce you to Bobbie. Bobbie is an inspiring, high energy person whom I had the opportunity to hear give a presentation on networking and collaboration at a Black Women in Business (BWIB) meeting. Since networking is something I teach in my seminars, there was a natural connection. We decided to meet, get to know one another, and then explore ways we might be able to help each other.

We have been challenged in our women's business group to change the atmosphere when we enter a room. Bobbie does just that. She was my two p.m. appointment the same day I met Kendal from Chapter 4. Bobbie has a fun personality; what comes across to me is that she knows who she is and is confident in that.

Bobbie is married and has a furry facet to her family—a dog and a cat. Her background is in physical education. As she was learning more about the school system while in college, she became aware that the teaching field was not what she initially thought it would be. Bobbie decided that with all of the red tape and testing required, the school system would not allow her to fulfill her vision and mission of making an impact on students' health and fitness. She decided to go back to school to learn about nonprofit management. It was only natural for her to combine her skills and interests to become the founder of Jamsz Konnections, a 501(c)(3) event planning organization with a passion for serving the nonprofit community. They help other 501(c)(3) nonprofit companies that are committed to health and fitness build their capacity by organizing fundraising events on their behalf. You can connect with her at www.jamskonnections. org. Please, meet Bobbie.

My friend, Jackie, introduced me to her friend, Diane, who was in Austin for a brief visit. Diane was born in the great state of Maryland, just like me. She is a wife and a mother to her daughter, Kathryn. You'll never guess what she does for a living: she is a pilot. Hers is a story of overcoming obstacles to achieve her dream of flying.

Diane first wanted to go into the military to fly but was disqualified from being able to fly for the Air Force because of their strict eyesight qualifications. Her recruiter told her to sign up anyway, and they would see what they could do to get a waiver. Warning! Warning! If it is not in writing, do not believe it. Proceed at your own risk. Take it from a former Air Force contracting person; once you sign on the dotted line, the military will hold you to what you agreed to in writing!

Thankfully, Diane did not take the bait. Instead, she strategically went to work as a flight attendant so she could ask the pilots a lot of questions. She already had an associate degree and her private pilot's license. She worked as an attendant for a while, then began working toward becoming a pilot for the airlines. She worked and borrowed every penny she could to go back to school to earn her bachelor's degree and her pilot ratings. However, Diane ran into a roadblock. She had her multi-engine license but without experience could not rent a plane to get the hours needed to fly for the airlines, yet she could not get the necessary experience without being able to rent a plane.

To earn some flight hours, Diane spent a year working as a flight instructor. She shared that she moved back in with her family because the pay as an instructor was unexceptional. She then took a part-time traffic flying job to earn additional hours: flying a news traffic reporter all over D.C. during early morning traffic.

While Diane was doing the traffic job, she was also working a desk job to support herself. She would fly for three hours in the morning, then be at her desk job by ten a.m. She also flew aerial photography flights for free to build up time. She told me that in 1999, for a solid year, she flew traffic watch in the morning, worked her desk job, then if it was a clear day, she would fly aerial photography. The time away from the desk to fly aerial photography had to be made up, so she would complete her desk job hours on the weekend. That year she only had two days off for the entire year: Christmas was one of those days.

Diane finally completed the 1,500 flight hours and 250 multi-engine hours she needed to apply to the airlines. She said that at one point, she thought her dream would never happen, and there was a physical ache in her heart at the thought of not flying. Today she is a pilot for Jet Blue. Her persistence and determination won the day. Please, meet Diane and her daughter, Kathyrn.

I would like to introduce you to Vicki, a homeschool settler. She homeschooled her two daughters for sixteen years straight and started right after it became legal to do so. She informed me that those who originally started the homeschool movement are called pioneers; her group, which came right after the pioneers, is considered settlers. She and her husband served on the board of a support group leading other families numbering between 80-140 families, depending on the year.

Since I homeschooled my children too, I felt a strong connection to Vicki and a deep admiration for what she had accomplished. In case you are interested, the folks in my group of homeschoolers—which came later and after various legal questions were settled—are considered tourists, which I think is appropriate. By comparison, I am sure it was relatively smooth sailing for my group.

By the time I was homeschooling, there were plenty of established curricula from which to choose. States had developed guidelines for homeschooling parents, and co-ops existed where parents could come together to teach specific subjects. There were organized groups for children to have adequate socialization, proms, and even graduation exercises. I don't know that I could have done what the pioneers and settlers did, paving the way and teaching too.

Vicki was a lawyer doing general litigation when she felt a tug at her heart to be home with her eighteen-month-old daughter. While being a stay-at-home parent is hard work and not for everyone, Vicki says she enjoyed it very much. She loved her time teaching her children.

Vicki is originally from Belleville, Illinois and lived there until she was thirty when her husband received a promotion. Vicki is a person of faith and says that when they initially moved from Belleville to Decatur, Illinois for the promotion, it was her new church community that helped her get through the rough time of being homesick. She later moved to a small town with no restaurants, so she had to learn to cook. She has lived in several places since then, including sunny Florida.

After graduating her children from school, Vicki went back to work, but not as a lawyer initially; instead, she tried her hand at many jobs. She has held various types of positions over the years and found that she enjoyed teaching; she once worked as an ESL teacher in the inner-city community for adults. Vicki has even written an adult literacy curriculum. One of the jobs she held was clerking for a judge and working in the legal library, preparing documents for people who could not afford lawyers. She found a lot of that work fascinating, and she eventually did go back to practicing law for a time.

Vicki is now a grandmother. She and her husband moved to Austin to be close to one of their daughters and grandson. They travel back to Illinois to see their other daughter and her husband and to help them with building their house and other things. Vicki's husband spent some of his professional life as a home builder. Vicki is very close to her daughters and values being able to contribute to their lives. I was able to glean invaluable nuggets of wisdom from her. Please, meet Vicki.

I was sure I had a meeting with the wife of a friend of mine, Melinda. I introduced her to you already in Chapter 3. However, I arrived at her office a little early: twenty-four hours early, to be exact. I did what I'm sure you would have done in my shoes; I went a couple of doors down in the same business complex to a store called The Rural Home. There, I met Laurie and Renée. I introduced myself, told them about my project, and we had a fantastic conversation.

Renée and Laurie met at a wine social hour and hit it off right away; they were the only women in the group still working, and they both came from upstate New York. When they started talking, they found they connected. One thing led to another, and now they work together. They jokingly call themselves Thing One and Thing Two. Renée says they're "sort of the 1+1 = 3 kind of women." They focus on different areas of the business and have a great time working together. While Renée focuses on their social media and business relationships, Laurie is the leader in design.

LAURIE'S STORY:

Laurie is a decorator, designer, and co-owner of The Rural Home. She had a full career in the corporate world as an oil and gas industry accountant. When Laurie retired, she decided to follow her passions as a creative force. She has owned her shop for more than twenty years and is affectionately called The Vortex. If you come into her store, ask her how she got her nickname; you won't regret it. Laurie is married, has two children and three grandchildren, (soon to be four at the writing of this book).

Laurie enjoys what she does. She also enjoys going into people's houses and helping them make it a home. The original name of her shop was The Rural House, but she said a house plus love equals a home, so she changed the name to The Rural Home.

Laurie grew up on a farm in upstate New York. Her family did not have a lot of material wealth, but they had each other. Raised with a strong work ethic, she has worked since she was nine years old. Her grandmother was very instrumental in her life, teaching her about history by taking her to old museums and acting as Laurie's tour guide. These excursions with her grandmother were a welcomed break from farm work and school. She enjoyed making crafts with her mother and her three older sisters. Now that she has The Rural Home, her sisters and mom will send her some of their crafts to sell; in this way, it's a family affair.

Her mom just turned ninety; she and her sisters celebrated their mother by taking her on a trip to Mexico. Her mother told her the secret to staying vibrant is always to stay curious about life and learning. One way Laurie does that is through the conversations she has at her shop. More on the shop later.

RENÉE'S STORY:

Renée is trained as a dietician. She ran an undergraduate program at the University of Buffalo where she was the coordinator and taught fifteen credit hours each semester. When her sister moved to Florida, she picked up her bags and moved to be closer to her sister and nephews. There was another perk that happened with this move—she met her future husband. Her family was complete, except for the two dogs and two cats they later adopted.

In Florida, Renée transitioned from teaching into corporate America. Her last corporate role was in healthcare as the Vice President of a small health technology company. Her job went virtual, which gave her tremendous flexibility. When her husband expressed his desire for a change of scenery, they came up with a short list of possible locations: Austin happened to be at the top of the list. It only took a brief five-day visit for Renée to fall in love with Austin, and they moved here two months later.

Once settled, Renée decided being a Vice President and the twelve to fourteen-hour days had lost their appeal. She felt like a change was in order. Her sentiments were, "You do what you have to early in your career to make money, then you do what fills your soul, later." It was about this time she met Laurie. A little over a year ago, Renée became co-owner of The Rural Home. She still does a little corporate consulting on the side.

What I found charming about these two women was their warmth. They did not talk to me about the items in their store; they spoke to me about the people who walked through the door and the necks they hugged. They told me the story of the seventy-three-year-old man and the sixty-year-old woman that had been together for twenty years who finally got married, and how they felt honored to have been invited to the wedding. The woman had been a customer of theirs. They told me about the lady who came in sad on two separate occasions, and when they asked her how she was doing, she shared she had recently lost her son. That day the three of them sat and cried together. They spoke of a customer who refused to tell them her name the first time she visited the shop, then reluctantly gave her name on the second visit. She opened right up on her third time in the shop after Laurie called her by name. Their philosophy is "They come as strangers, but they leave as friends." To these two ladies, they're in the business of people. You can find out more about them on their Facebook page at www.facebook.com/TheRuralHome. In the meantime, please meet Laurie and Renée.

Thanksgiving was over and the holiday season in full swing; I wanted to get a jump on my holiday shopping. I decided to go shopping to buy an ingredient for my Christmas mocha mix, and I met two wonderful store employees. Well, I met four, but I got to hear the stories of just two of them: Ria and Lory. Let me tell you about Ria.

My challenge resonated with Ria because her philosophy is, "Everybody lives their life and has a story that should be written." Originally from Houston, she moved to Austin, which she enjoyed. While in Austin, Ria relished her career as a chef where she ran entire kitchens. After she entered the industry, she discovered it was a man's world. To overcome and adapt to her surroundings, she admits she became a "man-woman kind of thing." She feels like she mastered her role as a chef, but it took its toll after fifteen years.

Ria had to move from Austin to Dripping Springs to take care of her parents. Relocating to Dripping Springs and becoming a caregiver, Ria needed to have a break from her demanding career and pursue something she could do for the long-haul. So, she has taken a less demanding job; in her off time, she has turned her attention to becoming a farmer and gardener.

Fairy gardening is her thing: for those that need to look that up like I had to, it's the art of creating miniature decorative gardens. Ria is quite proud of the fact she is now part of the garden movement and is trying to become a National Master Gardner. She is "reformatting" her passion from the cooking to the gardening aspect of food. Ria thinks it is essential to know what's happened to that tomato you are going to eat. She believes that by working as a farmer and gardener, she is going after her dream (versus someone else's) while pursuing living a healthy lifestyle.

Ria calls herself "a very simple girl." She is married. Ria doesn't have any children but has quite a few animals to take care of—dogs, cats, chickens, and sometimes goats. She emphasized she is loving life and trying to feed people the right way. When I asked her if she would like to share anything else, she very lightheartedly gave a "Woohoo! Let's all get along and have a beautiful world out there. God bless us all!" With that, please, meet a very cheery Ria.

My friend, Nicole, was hosting an event called The Gallery of Self-Doubt. Many of her friends came out to view and hear her talk about her art. One of those friends was Patrice. Patrice is from Manhattan, New York. She still has a brother that lives on the east coast. Patrice lived in Manhattan for twenty-seven years, then moved to Woodstock, New York. Before Woodstock became known for music, it was an art colony, and art is Patrice's second love. Her first love is ballet. She studied at Julliard for nine years to become a prima ballerina; when she didn't make it as a ballerina, she turned her attention to art.

From New York, she went to graduate school in Ohio for art education. She has done 3-D art sculptures, murals, and a few illustrations. From Ohio, she moved to the mountains of Colorado, and the state of Washington. Then she moved to the Texas Hill Country, where she has lived for the past twenty-two years.

Patrice has always enjoyed working with her hands. Today she does therapeutic massage and mainly concentrates on Ayurvedic massage, which is an integrative modality that balances the body and mind through the medium of oil.

Continuing with the theme of working with your hands, Patrice also enjoys woodworking. She shared that she used to be involved with construction and built shelters with Habitat for Humanity; she has very diverse talents. As her mother was a pastry chef, she also quite naturally developed a love for cooking.

Patrice has, in her words, fur babies: a couple of dogs and a cat she enjoys taking for walks. She enjoys eclectic groups of people and has developed a taste for a variety of music; in addition to ballet music, she listens to classical and jazz. Please, meet Patrice.

I met Sheri at Dunkin' Donuts. She is originally from Chicago but moved to Miami, Florida when she was twelve. After high school, she attended college for a little while in Miami but eventually moved to Austin; there is more than one way to earn an education. Sheri found her way on to the opening team of the Central Market HEB grocery store as the bakery manager. Her mother was proud of her.

Sheri had to overcome quite a few challenges early on in her life. At the age of sixteen, she was diagnosed with juvenile rheumatoid arthritis. Faced with the prospect of using a wheelchair for life, she was put on experimental drugs. The drugs did not work, and in her young adulthood, she made some choices that were not so good. Thankfully, Sheri realized she needed a real change; she moved to Austin, where she had a high school friend. That was forty-two years ago, and she says it was an excellent move. Two of the young people she had previously hung around were deceased two years after she left Miami.

Sheri successfully turned her life around. Instead of depending on drugs of any kind, including aspirin, she focuses on eating healthy and exercises every day. She now feels better than she did while she was on medication. All these many years later, she's still wheelchair free.

Professionally, Sheri has held several positions. For ten years, she was a scratch baker (a baker that bakes from individual ingredients vs. pre-mixes) for Dunkin Donuts. Next, she started her own video business. Then, she became a mother; her daughter is her pride and joy. After returning to work, she went to work for HEB Central Market as the bakery manager for thirteen years. Her next move was to open a café called Eat Dessert First. Unfortunately, Sheri was only able to keep this business viable for five years. However, it was a good turn of events. She was able to be there for her mother when her mother became ill and had to go through chemotherapy and radiation treatments. She cared for her mom during the last six months of her life then went back to work for Dunkin Donuts for a second time until she finally retired.

The Dunkin Donuts franchise owners have a lot of confidence in Sheri. They called her back from retirement for a third stint—this time to be the marketing coordinator for all ten stores. Her responsibilities also include taking care of corporate orders, special orders, and grand openings.

Sheri loves gardening, baking, and exercising, but what she is most proud of is the volunteer work she does for the Texas Organ Sharing Alliance. She spends time educating people about organ donation. She donated a kidney to her mom; ironically, she had the surgery on Mother's Day. Because of Sheri's sacrifice and that of one of her aunts, Sheri's mom lived another twenty-one years and had the opportunity to meet seven of her grandchildren. She wants everyone to know there is a program called pair matching. Instead of a patient having to have a family member as an exact match, several patients and family members can be mixed and matched. You can learn more about this life-saving program at www.kidney.org/transplantation/livingdonors/incompatiblebloodtype. Please, meet Sheri.

I had a dentist appointment, and they had recently hired a new dental technician, Brenda, who was taking care of me. I found out she was born in Austin, but both of her parents are from Mexico. Brenda has been married for three years and has two younger sisters. Her husband was born in Mexico and is in the process of getting his resident card. So far, it has taken two years, and they expect it to be another one-and-a-half-year wait.

After high school, Brenda volunteered and was eventually hired to work at Austin Fairy Godmother Boutique—a non-profit shop providing prom dresses, wedding gowns, and formal accessories for rent at reasonable prices. For the three years after that, she worked in the health, beauty, and food services industries. Brenda enjoyed having regular hours that mirrored her husband's work schedule. Brenda finally decided on the dental field because she had always had good experiences at the dental office over the years. Once the decision was made to enter the field of dentistry, she started classes in December and graduated in March. As part of her program, she had to do an externship; she completed a portion of her externship with my dentist, Tucker Family Dentistry.

Her training taught her the basics, of course, but she appreciated having the opportunity to see the whole process, including patient contact. Brenda believes she learned the most by actually applying the principles she had been learning. It turns out she had been a patient of Dr. Tucker. She was quite happy to be able to do some of her service hours with Dr. Tucker, which then led to her current employment, and she told me she is pleased to be here.

Brenda enjoys going out with friends and traveling to see her six godchildren. I was surprised at the number of godchildren she has until I found out she is from a very tight-knit community. Her friends are the children of her parent's friends, and many of these friends are from the same town in Mexico. She has noticed that people in the U.S. often are born in one state but then disperse and don't see each other much. People from the same town in Mexico tend to live in the same communities together in the U.S., so they have tight community bonds and lots of family friends. She would like to travel to Florida and California one day as she has family there; eventually, she plans to visit Greece. Please, meet Brenda.

I met Kirk at our mutual friends Paul and Cyndy's home. Kirk
is from Houston but also lived in Dallas and Austin as a young
boy. He is the oldest of three, having a younger brother and sister, both of whom he holds in high esteem. He started his high
school career with straight A's, but then he chose to hang out
with a bad crowd. He was thrown in jail at the age of sixteen for
being a runaway, and his parents had to come to get him out.
Kirk would butt heads with his father, and he was considered
the black sheep of the family. Instead of mending his ways, he
continued to feel entitled—that is, until his youth minister was
honest with him and told him, "You're a real screw up." Somehow,
that got through to him. He said he went from having no friends
to the wrong friends to being the president of the church camp.
By the end of his senior year, he was getting straight A's again.

After high school, Kirk began his college career at Baylor.
He later transferred to the University of Texas because of their
architectural program. Kirk married his wife, Donna, during
the fourth year of his five-year program; she put him through
his last year of school. Following graduation, he had a couple
of jobs with increasing responsibility which necessitated moves
from Houston, TX to Richmond, Virginia, to Denver, Colorado
and finally back to Austin, Texas. Along the way, Kirk became

the father of twins: a boy and a girl. In 2000, he started his own company, called PARC, LLC, doing architectural consulting on parking projects. You can find out more about his company at www.parkingdesign.info.

In 2008, the company had nineteen employees and was doing exceptionally well. Then the stock market crashed, and commercial lending stopped, which meant commercial developments also saw a significant decline. In December of 2008, his company billed $250K for work—in January of 2009, only $20K. Instead of a slow business decline, it was a cliff. And it didn't get better. In hindsight, he described going through this experience as healthy but painful. "I feel much less entitled now, which is probably a theme for how I kind of feel about life in general at this point." Since there wasn't much work, he decided to go back to school and studied church history at Trinity Evangelical Divinity School while consulting part-time. It was the same year his twins started their freshman year in college; while his daughter stayed in Texas for school, his son went to school in Chicago. That worked out great for Kirk because his school was also in Chicago. He got to watch his son play freshman football while learning more about pre-reformation justification by faith alone, which he found fascinating.

After spending two semesters in college and living on campus, Kirk returned to Austin and became a global mission's pastor for two years. He loved seeing the things God was doing in Africa. He spent time in the Dominican Republic, an area now considered South Sudan, and Kigali, Rwanda. Kirk enjoyed being in the field of world missions. In Rwanda, he learned a new definition of what it means to have no sense of entitlement.

"They're trying to find their next meal, and you've never met a people more generous, more loving, who are depending on each other living in a community. It's great to be in with the people where you can see God tangibly: people grateful for their blessings. [It is] miraculous that people could live, work, love, and trust each other on the heels of 800,000 people being killed in ninety days. Everybody you meet had lost someone: the warmest people that are grateful. They're grateful to be alive."

His business did pick back up enough to support his family, but he chose not to have employees; having to let people go was hard. His perspective has changed over the years. Kirk says that at sixty, he has much better boundaries than he did when he was working twenty-hour workdays before the market crash and that he feels incredibly blessed. "Today, I don't market. I have no delusions about where my opportunities come from. I try to be a good steward of God-given opportunities, and for me, marketing is answering the phone."

"I love riding Uber—because I meet people from all over the world—and being counter-cultural." Kirk also shared with me that he loves, "popping bubbles and preconceptions about old white guys." He enjoys learning the driver's stories. He was talking to one lady who was from Ghana. She was a chef that drove Uber as a second job. He asked her if she was going home for the holidays. She said, "No. Gay daughters don't get along with traditional family."

He told her, "My faith tells me to love you regardless of situation or circumstance." He said he left her a generous tip and she was just slack-jawed that this old white guy, who loved Jesus, wasn't condemning her. He didn't feel she had been extended a lot of love. He said, "It's kinda fun to love on an Uber driver." Kirk likes woodworking and reading. In particular, he enjoys reading westerns and theology. Please, meet Kirk.

My friend, Catharine, introduced me to Dani. They both love horses, and that is how they connected. Dani is a mortgage loan officer certified in working with Veterans Affair loans, so Catharine thought it would be good to connect the two of us. Dani may be able to pass along valuable information I could share in my military transition seminars. I'm all ears anytime I get the chance to learn information that may be useful in my workshops. So, we met for tea. I ordered hot, and she ordered cold.

Dani was born and raised in Norco, California. She informed me that there are more horses per capita in that city than any other city in the U.S., and that is where she developed her love for them. Dani is married and has a son. She also has an older sister and two older brothers. She specifically mentioned being close to her sister, who is ten years her senior. The story goes that her grandmother loaned a gentleman seventy-five dollars. When he couldn't pay it back, her grandmother settled for a pony instead. Her grandmother gave her that pony when she was three, and her thirteen-year-old sister taught her how to ride it. Dani developed a passion for horses from that first pony and still rides today. She did mention there was a "slight" ten-year gap in her love of riding. Can you guess when that was?

If you guessed that the gap occurred in high school when she became interested in boys and cars, you would be correct. Dani still had a horse for a while even after she got married at nineteen, but she eventually gave it to her niece. She didn't get another horse until she was twenty-six. After high school, Dani went immediately to work for a title company. She started back when title searching was done using microfiche recordings. She was diligent and set out to learn all of the facets of this profession. She worked there for just over a year when the company laid her off. At this point, she decided to get her real estate license and that she would not work for a huge company again. They had laid her off so they could pull from another company. She saw the politics of it all and decided she would be better off on her own. She has been a sole proprietor ever since.

Dani sold real estate for six months, and then she was in a car accident that resulted in her being on crutches for six months. Since she was unable to get around to show houses, she learned how to process loans, which she could do from a desk. It was valuable training for her. Dani decided to become a loan officer because now she had a unique skill set. She could package a loan, qualify the buyer, and calculate income from tax returns, so she was more valuable to her clients. "I was not just an order taker that turned over everything to someone that did the paperwork. I did it all: from start to finish." You can find out more information about her loan services at www.facebook.com/PanaceaMortgage.

I asked her what brought her to Austin. Her husband and his father had owned a manufacturing plant in California, and she had accompanied her husband on several business trips to Texas. As they got to know the area, they fell in love with it; Dani and her husband knew they were going to land somewhere in Texas eventually. In 2006, there were a lot of home buying opportunities, so they bought several properties in Texas. They sold some, rented some, and flipped some; by 2008, they loaded up the truck, and they moved to Beverly. By that I mean they sold their manufacturing plant and flew to Texas.

In addition to horseback riding, Dani enjoys singing and loves fashion. She loves fashion so much that she once owned a boutique called Ranch to Runway but found it took too much time away from her mortgage loan business. That doesn't stop her from shopping, though. But the time she smiled the biggest was when she talked about her three-year-old grandson; her eyes just lit up. Please, meet Dani.

6

Why Not?

"Some men see things as they are and ask why. I dream of things
that never were and ask why not."

—Robert Kennedy

Have you ever stopped to ask yourself, "Why not?" I
found it very refreshing amongst people in their twenties and thirties and wondered when I stopped asking
that question. Then, I began to wonder if I had ever really asked
that question. When I was in my twenties, I was in the military.
I followed a lot of rules and regulations, so there were not a lot
of options or opportunities at the junior ranks to take a calculated risk. I also got married young and started a family. When
you have responsibilities like that, there is not a lot of room for,
Why Not? The answer to that question is because I have responsibilities, plain and simple. But now that I am no longer in the
military and my children are grown, I find myself fascinated
by that question, so much so that five years ago, I started my
coaching and public speaking business. I have found it to be
quite liberating and exciting.

Don't get me wrong, I don't think one should throw all caution to the wind, but if you are using wisdom and taking a calculated risk, why not? It is useful to do an assessment occasionally of where you are to see if you are holding onto a limiting belief that no longer applies. I realized I am living my *"Why not?"* but just a bit later after I raised my children.

I had lunch with Erin, who lives in my neighborhood. We met through the app Nextdoor. When I signed up for the app, she was kind enough to reach out to welcome me. I asked her if she would be willing to meet for lunch. She was open to the idea, and why not since we are neighbors? Granted, you must use a bit of caution when meeting a stranger; you fill out a profile on the app, and we met during the day in a public location. Within a few moments of talking with her, I could tell she has a mind for business.

Erin started out wanting to be in hotel management but later thought better of it. She did not believe the hours would be conducive to how she wanted to raise her family. She loves accounting but spends the bulk of her work focusing on running her business: Modern Mobile Notary. If you need a notary to come to your door, consider getting in touch with her at modernmobilenotary@gmail.com.

Erin is from California and has two younger brothers and an older sister. She is a wife and mother of two and lights up when she talks about her sons. Erin is affable, authentic, has an optimistic personality, and is passionate about family. She spoke fondly of her siblings and her parents. You can sense their closeness even though her immediate family still lives in California. She is grateful that she does have some family close by too. Erin has unique nicknames in her family: Tomato and Jams or Jamin. Very colorful, and I'll bet that will start a few conversations in the future. She enjoys her church and the connections she has made there. Erin also shared that she has an interest in hunting.

We discussed family, faith, and business; we also "discussed" the importance of healthy eating, while we enjoyed our giant burgers and fries. Please, meet Erin.

I encountered two young ladies on my walk. They were both pushing strollers for little ones, but not their own; they are au pairs. Meet Ana and Summer.

Ana is eighteen years old and is from Mexico. She is taking one year off before she goes to college as she tries to decide what she wants to do professionally. She knows she loves kids, so being an au pair fits her perfectly. Ana has a very youthful, carefree spirit. She has only been in the U.S. for one month; this is her first time out of her country.

Ana says the food is super-sized, and she is very conscious of the sugar content. Our "small" drink size is a large back in Mexico. She had heard about America since she was a little girl, but Ana thought the things she was hearing were not real; Ana got here and realized much of what she had heard was indeed true. She has already been to New Jersey, New York, and now Texas. She hopes to take a road trip before going home to see a lot more of America.

I was introduced briefly to Summer a year ago when I was visiting with my friend and her new baby. Summer is a pediatric nurse from China; she's twenty-six years old. She has extended her time here for another year. I asked her what she had discovered about America, and she answered with one word. "Freedom." In China, she would be expected to be married or getting married soon; she does not feel that pressure here.

While open to trying different American foods, Summer prefers authentic Chinese. She says, "Americans like sweet food." When she returns to China, she hopes to take a year to travel around China. She thinks she will have the flexibility to do this because her profession of being a nurse will always be in demand. Please, meet Ana and Summer.

I met three very courageous and adventurous people at the library of all places. For now, I want to talk to you about Sarah. Sarah is originally from Baytown, Texas. She has three older brothers, one older sister, and one younger sister. Her sisters are five years apart on either side. I asked her what it was like to grow up with five siblings. She said, "Chaotic," but her brothers did move out after a while as they were quite older.

Sarah was homeschooled for high school and went to community college in Baytown to get her associates degree in English. She later attended Texas State and completed her degree in English with a minor in history. Sarah described herself as quiet and shy but was quite comfortable in the library. Growing up, she always loved books and going to the library.

Right after college, Sarah took a job in the insurance industry. As you can imagine, she did not love it. You may be as surprised as I was to learn that Sarah, as shy as she was, decided to go on a mission trip to Indonesia. She went to Medan, Sumatra. Google says Medan has a population of 2.2 million people, but Sarah felt sure it was much, much larger than that because it felt so packed. She also told me that the driving was crazy there; people drove within millimeters of each other, yet she never saw a single accident.

Sarah loved Indonesia and feels as though she left a piece of her heart there. She said the Indonesian people are wonderful and happy and welcomed her into their homes. Those she encountered had never met people from America, so Sarah and her group were treated like celebrities. Everyone wanted to take their picture. When she would look up from eating, she would often catch people filming her. Talk about living in a fishbowl! The people of Sumatra called them bulé, which means foreigner.

I was impressed that Sarah dared to go to a foreign country and even more impressed that she thrived under the microscope of cameras after candidly sharing with me that she developed agoraphobia while in high school. She credits taking dual credit courses, and speech in particular, for helping to open her up. I think she is courageous to have faced this fear and conquered it. We all have phobias; mine is a fear of heights. To be afraid and do something anyway is the very definition of courage, and I applaud her.

Two days after Sarah came back from her trip, she left the insurance job and soon found her current position at the library as an assistant. She is planning to go back to school to get her Master of Library Science and has her sights set on becoming a librarian.

For fun, Sarah knits, reads, and writes. She has written commentaries as well as nonfiction, and she is currently writing a young adult novel. Sarah is a delightful and amazing person who has overcome challenges that only a determined individual could. She is a person of action, and I am sure she will accomplish anything she sets her sights on. Please, meet Sarah.

Joel had a new TV installed in our living room. Joel had scheduled it to be done, but he was nowhere to be found when Andrew and Joshua showed up, so, it was my lucky day. I got the chance to meet two nice young men. I will tell you about Andrew first and Joshua next.

Andrew has two brothers and three sisters and is a native of Austin. After graduating from high school, he went out to look for work and, in his words, "fell into this industry." He learned it the old-fashioned way with on-the-job training. Andrew enjoys meeting new people every day, so he still finds his job very interesting.

I asked him what his hobbies were, and he told me his children. His children are five, six, eleven, and twelve. He explained in more detail that he is into the things that excite his kids. He said when he was a child, his dad worked too much. It was good that he was able to provide for them, but he wished his father could have been around more. In light of that, one of his favorite places to go to is called the Main Event. He was surprised I had not heard of it. To listen to him tell it, it is a magical place. The energy in his voice changed when he was describing it to me. I learned the Main Event has an arcade, pool tables, bowling, rock climbing, and laser tag; it also has an excellent area for the adults to mingle. Andrew cherishes time with his kids.

Both Andrew and Joshua were very thoughtful and customer-oriented as they helped me think through the placement of the TV. The best part for me was that in our conversation before my interview, we were talking about getting ready for the holidays. I learned Andrew had only heard of, but never tasted, eggnog. Well, Joel just happened to have bought our first carton of the season, and I got the chance to introduce him to the non-alcoholic version. He liked it, of course. Please, meet Andrew.

Now, I am going to tell you about Joshua. He is the sort of person that is a free spirit and not at all what I would have thought by my first impression. Joshua was born in Mesa, Arizona, just outside of Phoenix. He is from a Mormon family, so not surprisingly, he is one of seven. He has a younger brother and five younger half-sisters. His father died in a motorcycle accident, and his mother later remarried to "the greatest guy ever": Joshua's exact words.

Joshua's family moved to Colorado when he was ten. There he lived on a seventy-six-acre farm right next door to his grandfather's place. When I say farm, I mean it. He grew up milking cows every day before school. Often the grass is indeed greener on the other side of the fence. Joshua spent his younger years trying to get away from the farm. Now, in his thirties, he's trying to fight his way back to it. He just became the proud owner of a little piece of land outside of the city where he can own a few animals.

After high school, Joshua took random jobs and would work at each until he was bored. Then he would relocate to a new place. When Joshua left Colorado, he was on his way to South Carolina but stopped in Austin to see his brother; he fell in love with it and never left. He has had several different types of jobs, too, but what I found fascinating was the fact he didn't own a computer until eight years ago.

On top of that, he said he was not tech-savvy: he didn't even have an email address. After all, he did not need it on the farm. He never envisioned himself doing anything techy. He thought he'd be a trucker or something like that. Moving to Austin made him realize he was in a situation where he needed to learn or get passed by. He decided to learn.

Joshua spent hours getting frustrated, reading every instruction and every toolbar, and grinding through it. He jumped into a job he said was way over his head, but he was resolute and picked it up. Now Joshua enjoys working in this industry and is excited about how it is continually changing and growing. Joshua was laughing when he was telling me he can do tv installation, security systems, cameras, wiring for audio, wiring for your shades to go up and down: basically, make all things automatic and all at the press of one button, if you have the cash to roll like that. He's come a long way and knows it's been a huge, positive turnaround in his life.

Joshua is the proud papa of a five-month-old baby girl named Larue. And you would never guess it, but his hobbies are drawing, guitar, and sculpture work—anything artsy—and yes, let us not forget live streaming TV. Please, meet Joshua.

I introduced you to Matt in Chapter 2. I mentioned he has a brother, Joshua, who was with him to pick up my friend, Megan. Did you honestly think I would let the chance to meet someone new slip by?

Joshua is three years younger than Matt and has high regard for his big brother. Joshua consulted him when making his college and career choices. He told Matt that he was good at and liked math and physics; naturally, Matt recommended Texas A&M. Joshua attended Blinn for a year before joining his brother at school, and they lived together for three years.

Joshua studied civil engineering. After doing a couple of internships, he took a job in Austin working for the state doing bridge inspections; he climbs on bridges and hangs on the underside. A picture of Spiderman comes to mind. All I know is, I couldn't hang off such heights, but he thinks it's pretty cool.

For fun, Joshua has several hobbies: he likes playing softball, volleyball, and Frisbee. He also enjoys motorcycle riding and hunting. I'm noticing an outdoor theme. Please, meet Joshua.

Joel and I were visiting some good friends who had recently moved. While Joel helped our friend, Buck, clear some overgrown brush, I went with his wife, Lisa, to check out the jewelry at a Noonday party across the street. I met the Noonday ambassador, Laura, and the hostess, Amy. I will tell you about Laura, and then I am going to tell you a little about Noonday because of its global impact.

Laura moved to Austin with her mother, father, and brother when she was five, so she considers Austin home. Being an Austinite for so many years, she misses the small-town feel it used to have. Laura graduated from Texas A&M; so yes, she's an Aggie. She is married and has three children, ages eight, ten, and twelve: the older two children are sons, and their youngest is a daughter. Their eight-year-old came into their family through adoption from Rwanda, Africa.

Laura wanted to be a stay-at-home mom, but she was told her son would be better off if they could provide him with a private education where the class size is much smaller, and the day is simpler, as he has a few special needs. Wanting to provide a more suitable academic environment for her son, Laura knew she would need to work. When she and her husband were in the process of adoption, Laura happened to meet Jessica Honegger, who is the founder of the company Noonday. An opportunity came about for Laura to join Jessica's team. She has been there for five years now. Jessica's adopted son is from the same orphanage in Rwanda that Laura's daughter is from, so their children knew each other before Jessica and Laura knew their respective children.

Laura's passion is to advocate for people around the world. Visiting other countries, she has seen extreme poverty levels and feels great knowing she can play a small role in helping empower others. Laura loves to travel. In her work, she has traveled to Rwanda, Uganda, Ecuador, Peru, and Vietnam, and she will be going to Guatemala this summer. Traveling suits her just fine. When she has free time, she likes to go out with girlfriends or decorate her house.

Now to talk about Noonday.

Jessica started Noonday because she was trying to raise money to adopt their son. In the process of selling jewelry, purses, and accessories, Noonday eventually created 4,500 jobs for artisans in thirteen different countries and is now a fair-trade company, meaning everyone gets a fair wage and is treated with dignity.

There are three hundred people employed by Noonday in Uganda alone. Some of the workers are in the villages, and some are in the city of Kampala: eighty percent are single mothers. The founder, Jessica, has created a daycare for some of the single moms. That is unique because many impoverished countries do not have childcare systems, which makes it even harder for women to be sure their children are cared for while they work. Jessica also allows other moms to work from home rolling beads. That enables those moms to have a job and be stay-at-home moms like stay-at-home moms in the U.S. Laura said that when you travel to those countries, initially you feel the differences, but then you see we are so much the same. She calls it "The Sisterhood Across The Globe."

In some countries, there are specific groups that work to give women working in prostitution an alternative dignified job. They also provide work for men and women with HIV and women who are uneducated. According to Laura, "There is something that lifts your head when you are able to bring home a paycheck." If you would like to find out more about Noonday or are in the market for new accessories, why not check out the link below? In the meantime, please, meet Laura.

www.laurachoy.noondaycollection.com

Joel had the day off and treated me to a late lunch. The food was excellent and our server, Jenny was fantastic. She was the server for the table right behind us with two moms of one-and-one-half-year-olds; one of the moms, Elizabeth, fearlessly sat down beside Joel, complimented me on my hair and then asked our server for a particular drink. Elizabeth wasn't in a hurry for it but was asking very kindly. She popped in again later while running behind her little one and was so friendly, outgoing, and full of life. I knew I had to ask her and her friend for some of their time. I'll start by talking about Elizabeth.

Elizabeth was born in Orange, Texas, which is on the border between Texas and Louisiana, but grew up in Rockwall, Texas, just outside of Dallas. She is married and has a daughter and one older brother. Elizabeth made a point of telling me her daughter, Eleanor, is from Austin.

Elizabeth is well versed in the English language. She has an undergraduate degree in English from Texas A&M University-Commerce plus two master's degrees from the University of North Texas: one in English and one in teaching English as a second language. Elizabeth was working full-time then took off a year-and-a-half when her daughter was born but found she missed teaching. When she approached her school with a proposal to teach two days a week, they were open to it. Currently, she teaches English as a foreign language to adults part-time and loves it. Well, you never know unless you ask.

For fun, Elizabeth is in a group that plays board games. She reads sci-fi fantasy books, hosts trivia games once a week, and takes Eleanor on a lot of playdates. Before she had Eleanor, she performed in drag and burlesque but doesn't have time for that right now. She describes herself as an extreme extrovert, and there is every indication this is correct.

Elizabeth told me that she and Samantha are co-moms. I had never heard that term before, so I asked her to explain. She was quick to tell me they both have husbands. They met at a mom's playgroup and discovered they have very similar mothering styles and values. Since they both value the idea of children growing up with siblings but have decided to have only one child each, they are raising their girls as non-biological siblings. That's thinking outside of the box. Please, meet Elizabeth with Eleanor.

Now I will tell you about Elizabeth's friend and co-mom, Samantha, who was there with her daughter, Zoey. Samantha was born and raised in Austin, and she has an older brother and sister. She went to Austin Community College (ACC) to get the basics out of the way, earning her Pharmacy Technician certificate as well. After graduating from the pharmacy program, she was hired by a computer company. She worked at this company for a long time and met her husband there. Samantha has not yet put her pharmacy training to use but hopes to pursue employment that is related to her training in the future. She is also interested in going back to school, but for right now, she doesn't want to put her daughter Zoey, into daycare. In her free time, she likes to paint. Please meet Samantha and her daughter, Zoey.

Jenny was our server at lunch on the same day I met Elizabeth and Samantha. She posed the question, "Why not? This is the time." She went on to say that the societal expectation is to go to school, get a job, get married, buy a home, and have a family; Jenny has taken a different approach. Her opinion is that a lot of times people rush into a job, house, family, all so fast. She wonders, "What's the rush?" She decided she wasn't ready for a career just yet.

Jenny is from Evergreen, Colorado, a little mountain town about forty minutes west of Denver. When she graduated from the University of Denver in March of 2017, she was ready for something new, so she struck out hiking at the beginning of the summer. Jenny made it six hundred miles along a trail going from Mexico to Canada before she hurt her knee and had to stop. Still looking for adventure, she decided to move to Austin. She knew a couple of people here, found a job and declared, "It's been great so far." Not one to quit, she has plans to try completing the trail next summer.

Jenny's degree is in international development and health with a focus on the Middle East and Sub-Sahara Africa. She speaks some Arabic but learned the most while studying abroad in Jordan for four months. She loved it. "It's a culture we don't understand much as Americans, and there's a lot of stereotypes that go around the Middle East. That's not to say that there aren't some really bad things happening, but there are also incredible people with incredible history and a culture that you can't even begin to grasp until you immerse yourself in it." The reason Jenny chose to study Arabic was that school had always come easy for her, and she wanted to challenge herself. Jenny said she specifically asked herself, "What can I do to make this hard?" Well, she found her answer! She said learning Arabic was "really hard and a great experience at the same time." She hopes to return to Jordan and teach English while continuing to learn more Arabic.

Though her mom and dad are divorced, Jenny told us she has a great family. Her mom lives in Wyoming, and her dad is still in Evergreen, Colorado. She also has an older sister who lives in Colorado, too. After visiting with her for a bit, I would say she is a glass half full kind of person. She enjoys skiing and is going back home in January to experience a few trips flying down the white powder once again, probably even a couple of black diamonds. It is evident Jenny enjoys spending time outdoors. She is trying to get back into running, but if you were to ask her, Jenny would tell you that hiking and backpacking are her biggest passions right now. Please, meet Jenny.

I had a business meeting downtown at the Driskill Hotel—the oldest operating hotel in Austin. While waiting, I met Sidney, who was working at the check-in desk. Sidney is a transplant from Gig Harbor, which is south of Seattle, Washington. She moved to Austin four months ago for work. Sidney likes Austin a lot, describing it as a mix of San Francisco, Portland, and Seattle—not what she was expecting at all. She thought she was going to encounter strong accents, cowboy hats, and cowboy boots!

Before moving to Austin, Sidney managed a hotel in Gig Harbor for two years. Before that, she was in Bellevue at a different hotel. Sidney told me she rarely meets people who are originally from Austin. She has two sisters still in Washington, and all three of them went to Washington State University. Sidney earned a bachelor's degree in sociology with a minor in hospitality business management. She raved about their program and said, "It was the best story of my life going to school there." The students call Pullman, the University's location, God's Country because it is a rural campus. Historically, God's Country is a term that has been used to describe numerous areas around the world that are sparsely populated. During her time at Washington State University, Sidney was a part of the Greek life as a member of the Alpha Gamma Delta sorority.

Sidney loves to travel. She has been to Australia, South America, and Europe and wants to go to Asia and Africa next; she's checking the continents off of her list. Sidney appreciates experiencing different cultures and different types of foods, and she thinks it's fantastic to get to know people who come from different parts of the world. Growing up in the Pacific Northwest, she enjoys hiking and exploring in the mountains, swimming in the lakes, and hanging out on the beaches. Fun fact: Sidney lived in Sydney, Australia during the millennium. She had a family member that worked for a company sponsoring the Olympics, so her family moved there for a little over a month. Please, meet Sidney.

Joel and I went to dinner with our friends Jeff and Sheji at Tillie's. We had a great server named DeAubrey. Joel asked her where her name came from, and she had such an interesting response that I asked DeAubrey if she would meet me for coffee later in the week so I could share her story with you.

DeAubrey is originally from Las Vegas, Nevada and lived there until she moved to San Antonio where she completed high school. She is an only child. When she first moved to Texas, she found herself having discussions with the kids on the bus but getting a strange reaction, and she didn't know why: DeAubrey was simply telling the students about her family. Ninety percent of the population in Vegas relies on the hotels and casinos for work; there are craps dealers, blackjack dealers, poker dealers, etc. Her dad happened to be a poker dealer, so like many friends often did, she told them what her father did for a living. The problem was she spoke to them as if she was talking to someone in Las Vegas—she said he was a dealer. Finally, someone told her she probably should not tell people that. Perplexed, she asked why, and then they connected the dots. In Texas, being a dealer meant something totally different; they thought she meant that he was a drug dealer! He had worked at the famous Caesar's Palace and later at the Mirage. Context is everything.

After high school, DeAubrey studied medical billing and coding but went into the restaurant/service industry instead. When she was twenty-seven, she did seasonal work; she would go to Alaska in the summer and then go somewhere else like Hawaii or Illinois in the winter. She did that a couple of times before moving to Alaska for two years. Alaska may seem an odd choice until you know her history. She had grown up hearing lots of stories about it. Her great-grandfather went there in 1945 and became a homesteader. Two years later he sent for her great-grandmother, Ruby, her grandmother, who was twelve, and her great aunt who was ten. When he sent for them, her great-grandmother then had to drive the three thousand miles from New Mexico to Alaska on dirt roads. She made the front-page news as the first woman to ever drive that drive without the presence of a man. Along the way, men that were traveling the same road were making bets that she would end up in a ditch: she proved them all wrong.

DeAubrey told me her family is relatively small, and she is very close to her grandmother. "Nanna is my best friend on Earth!" Her grandmother used to pick her up from kindergarten, and they would walk home. Along the way, they would stop for ice cream. "We just hung out together, and we still do."

DeAubrey has lived in Texas since 2016 but plans to move back to Alaska for good in the spring. She thinks it is the most beautiful place she has ever been—better than Hawaii—"stunningly gorgeous," and has fallen in love with the scenery and people. There's plenty to do like hiking, fishing, and camping in the summer and snow sports in the winter. DeAubrey was able to find work there and quickly moved up into management in the service industry. In addition to her outdoor endeavors, she enjoys making jewelry, painting, and other crafts.

Here is how the name DeAubrey came to be. Legend has it that a man named Aubrey saved one of her ancestors eight generations ago and dating back to the Civil War. Her ancestor was so grateful, he promised to call his first son Aubrey, but then the man only had daughters—five of them—so the man feminized the name and named one of his daughters DeAubrey. The name then was passed on to each generation, only skipping one; and for the last four generations, it has been passed on to the first daughter born to that generation. Many people compliment her on it and say it is both unique and pretty. She told me it is a fun name and has told those who fancy it, "If you like the name, use it. It should be out there." Please, meet DeAubrey.

7

Intentional Givers

"We make a living of what we get. We get a life for what we give."

—Author Unknown: Often attributed to Winston Churchill

I have yet to meet a true giver who is regularly unhappy. Sure, they may have hard times, but they don't stay down for long. Giving brings joy to the giver. It is hard then to be a regular giver and be regularly unhappy. Not only did I experience this myself during the 100-day challenge, but there is science to back it up. In separate studies, Professor Michael Norton of the Harvard Business School, Professor Elizabeth Dunn of the University of British Columbia, and researchers from the University of Zurich found that those who gave were happier. Their research involved giving participants five to twenty dollars for the day. The participants could choose to spend the money in whatever way they pleased. They could keep it for themselves or give it away. Those that decided to give it away achieved higher levels of happiness.

Being a giver is not to be confused with being a person without healthy boundaries. I mention this because while there are some people who are predominantly intentional givers, there are also those who are predominantly takers, and then there are your

Covert Contractors—those that give and take to various degrees but predominantly operate with a motive. Here are the three groups the way I see them.

1) True givers will give what they can without any expectation of anything in return and often intend to give: like the 100+ people that contributed to this book. They reap the rewards of a release of the feel-good hormones serotonin and dopamine simply from the act of giving. Being a giver does not mean they cannot be a recipient of someone else's act of kindness, nor does it mean that they have a problem asking for help when they need or desire it. It merely means that when they give, they give without the expectation of return from the person to whom they gave. The giving doesn't come cloaked with a hidden "bill due upon demand." They give because they can—and let's face it—they give because it makes them feel good.

A word of caution: For some faithful givers, there can be the danger of being taken advantage of because takers will seek them out. In this scenario, the intentional giver should stop and assess the situation. Also, if you are in a close relationship with a taker, it might be healthy to ask yourself this question, "If I'm taking care of you, and you're taking care of you, then who's taking care of me?" Intentional givers need wisdom in their giving; otherwise, they can be hurt deeply. Intentional givers can also be the happiest among us.

2) Takers are looking for what they can get. There are various levels of takers. Some will take regardless of the cost to another, and some will take until their conscience is pricked. The bottom line is that takers are not looking for an opportunity to give. They will take until the other person stops giving, and then they will look for someone else. They are manipulative and conniving.

3) Covert Contractors form a group many people operate in, but perhaps the people in this category are not even conscious of the fact they behave this way. The thought process for this

group is, "I'll do this for you because I know you would do it for me," or "I will expect you to return the favor." People in this group do good things for others with the expectation that the person will then offer something of the same or similar value, but this is a covert contract; the expectation is neither agreed upon nor expressly stated. Being in this group sets one up for many disappointments. Having an expressed agreement of "I'll do this for you, and you'll do that for me" does not fall into this category. That arrangement is called a contract and is a separate thing entirely.

Since everything is not black and white, there will be some cross over between the true giver and the covert contractor, depending on the situation or perhaps the people involved. The taker will operate predominantly as a taker, yet with certain people or on particular occasions be a giver. It's a heart issue. The question then becomes, "What are a person's intentions or motivations the majority of the time?" The folks in this chapter are intentional givers.

I had a very warm meeting with Drucilla, a woman who attends my church. When I walked through the door, we smiled at each other and said hello. We made the casual remark of it being a bit cold which progressed to a discussion of how we both carry sweaters everywhere, even during the summer—in Texas, when you come inside, the AC can be overwhelming. We hit it off right away. I saw her again after the service, and we decided to meet later to get to know one another.

We met at Austin Java. As we ordered our coffee, I discovered she likes cold brew. I have seen this in the coffee shops but had never ordered it because I thought it was always a cold drink: I was wrong. I learned a lot from her about how to make the drink.

Drucilla has a very unusual name. She told me her father read it in a book once and "liked it." She is very easy to talk to and has a captivating smile. Drucilla has been married for thirty-nine years and is delighted with her choice! She has a son and daughter and eight grandchildren whom she will gladly watch as needed; she said she is granny-on-call.

Drucilla was a teacher for twenty-five years and taught from pre-school to high school. Her favorite was high school, but she remarked that you take the available job. I learned that it was her high school biology teacher who inspired her to teach. She said this particular teacher left her with her mouth open (in amazement) every day. To all the teachers reading this, I think you have one of the most critical jobs on the planet!

At the very end of our meeting, I learned that Drucilla is involved with two prison ministries. One is the storybook ministry. The volunteers will bring books to the unit for an inmate to choose the story she wants to read out loud. They record the reading and mail it to the inmate's child; this makes me both happy and sad at the same time.

The other ministry Drucilla is involved with is Kairos Prison Ministry International. This ministry reaches out to impact the hearts and lives of incarcerated men, women, and youth, as well as their families, to become loving and productive citizens of their communities. This ministry goes in weekly, one time a month for a weekend with volunteers, and two times a year for a more substantial retreat. It is quite unique. You can read more about it at http://mykairos.org/. Please, meet Drucilla.

I had the pleasure of meeting Brenda at the movie theater. Joel and I had gone out to the movies and dinner with friends of ours. Upon my arrival, one of our friends, Patrick, greeted me warmly then told me he had someone he wanted me to meet; he knows I've been doing this challenge.

Brenda has been working at the same theater for eleven years. She has the perfect personality for a customer-facing position such as the one she was doing: taking everyone's tickets and telling them which way to go for their particular movie. My friend was even giving her a hard time, and she good-naturedly chided him with, "Patrick, are you being mean?" Anyone who can hold her own and give it right back to Patrick is a person after my own heart.

Joel dropped me off at the entrance and then parked the car. When he came in without tickets, Brenda asked him incredulously if he was making me buy the tickets. I liked her immediately. I can see why the theater asks her to be out front with the customers. I watched countless theatergoers' eyes light up when they saw her as they walked through the door. They greeted her by name with a very bright, "Hi, Brenda!"

Patrick later told me, "One of the reasons to go to the Arbor theater—other than art films—is to see Brenda. For over ten years, we've been regular patrons, and Brenda is the main feature. Regardless of whether we enjoyed the film, Brenda is the Academy award. She always smiles; she always jokes; she always makes you feel happy. Everyone who is a regular loves Brenda. She has an indelible loving personality." Please, meet Brenda.

I had the pleasure of meeting a beautiful family: Craig, Mandy, and Ellie. I was walking by their house when their four-year-old daughter, Ellie called out to ask me if I would like a cup of lemonade. Well, it is hard to resist a four-year old and lemonade. I didn't have any money on me since I was walking, but Mandy told me it was free!

The family was sitting at a turquoise table in their front yard. They were offering lemonade and cookies to those who passed. I was very intrigued, so I had to ask them what it was about. It turns out, there is a book written called *The Turquoise Table* that inspired them.

The book is about a lady named Kristin Schell who put an ordinary picnic table in her front yard, painted it turquoise, and began inviting friends and neighbors to join her. It changed life in her community and inspired my neighbors to do the same! Wow! I stumbled upon this young family seeking connection to their community! Of course, I had to take a couple of pictures to show you!

They are originally from Amarillo, TX, but moved to Austin 2 ½ years ago when Mandy's sister begged them to move closer. They were only 10 minutes away until Mandy's brother-in-law was later transferred to Nashville for work. Bummer! Mandy has two older sisters and a younger brother. She was a teacher for ten years and is now the Instructional Designer supporting other teachers for the Dripping Springs ISD. Her primary roles include the Learning and Innovation Coordinator, the Professional Learning Coordinator, and the Gifted and Talented Program Coordinator for her district.

Craig is a nurse. He is now the Director of Cardiovascular Services at St. David's South Austin Medical Center. Craig likes to run and is currently training for a triathlon. He was rather quiet and let Mandy do most of the talking.

Mandy said it is hard to get to know people with their busy lives. She had her tribe in Dallas but was finding it challenging to connect here. Mandy said it was hard even to see people who lived on the same street or get to know neighbors! She is on a mission to change all of that.

Mandy is planning to put a sign out in her yard to invite others to gather at her table even if they aren't around, hoping to create more community. She said she was looking for her thing and her tribe, and the turquoise table might be the answer to both! Perhaps it will inspire others to do the same. Please meet my neighbors: Craig, Mandy, and Ellie!

I decided to check out a cardio dance class to spice up my workouts, and I met Lauren, the dance instructor. She is very enthusiastic and has got some moves, I must say. She kept the class fun, which is essential for sure.

I have to admit, I was a bit tired, so I was not going to approach anyone in the class to meet them. I thought, *Oh, I'll just do it later.* As I was leaving the building, Lauren took the time to pause and say hello to me. She had her seven-year-old son, Charlie, with her. I asked her if she homeschooled, but she said no; Charlie just had the day off from school.

It turns out that being a cardio dance instructor is Lauren's decompression hobby. Now this will teach me not to make assumptions about people: Lauren is a full-time labor and delivery nurse. Teaching class keeps her accountable to her workouts. She also loves reading, yoga, and running outside. I asked her about yoga, in particular. She said it helps her to de-stress and balances out her workouts.

Lauren's parents and her brother also live in Austin. Her favorite things to do with Charlie are things that are adventurous and crazy like dancing in the rain. She also enjoys doing crafts with him. She shared that Charlie loves playing video games.

When I asked her why she enjoys nursing and leading classes, she revealed the common thread to me: she said her purpose in life is to help others, and she loves connecting with people. Lauren is certainly very good at that. Not only has she identified her life's purpose, but she is also living it.

Keep in mind that we had both just finished a tough workout. Somehow Lauren remained pretty fresh-looking. Charlie was quite shy, so I did not ask him for a picture. Please, meet Lauren.

I met Mary at Dede's house. I introduced you to Dede in Chapter 4; since that time, Dede and I have gotten together several times, and she has introduced me to several of her friends. Mary is married and has three grown sons, two of whom are married. Two of her sons live in the Washington, D.C. area, and one lives in Houston. Why is she not living in D.C., you may wonder.

Mary and her husband lived in Boston for thirty years but moved to Austin to be closer to their family—the son in Houston is the father of her two granddaughters. Ah-ha! There's the answer—grandchildren! Mary grew up in Houston; she is returning to her roots. She told me her parents and younger sister live in San Antonio, and she considers it a blessing to be close to family. She loves it here in Texas, and the climate suits her. She especially does not miss shoveling snow.

Professionally, Mary is an occupational therapist. Occupational therapy always came up as first or second on her aptitude tests in college, but because she did not know what it was, she didn't consider it until after she raised her family and decided to go back to work. Once she made the decision, Mary went back to school. She took the pre-requisite classes in her early forties at a community college then applied to occupational therapy school and got her master's degree in it.

Mary enjoyed what she was studying and said most days she finds her work very rewarding, but it can be challenging, too. Mary had done a lot of work with children over the years—she was once a piano teacher and had worked with preschoolers—so it was a natural fit for her to practice occupational therapy in the school system.

What she loves about her job is that she can work with a team to create environments conducive to learning for children who need additional help; some of her students need help dealing with only one challenge, while others are dealing with multiple situations.

Many schools will have special education teachers. Mary comes in, along with other specialists, to help support these teachers by designing different approaches or teaching methodologies suited to address student needs. I think of the impact she and others can have in the development of a child and the hope and encouragement this can be in the life of the parent of a special needs child.

As Mary described her job, I was struck by the level of compassion and patience that would be required to do this job well. With enthusiasm, she told me the rewards are there. This year, they will be working with a student to teach computer skills that will give the child a voice for the very first time. By pushing or looking at an icon, the computer will be able to speak for the student. What an opportunity for the child to communicate in a way never before possible!

Mary supports three school campuses. She emphasized that this work is done as part of a team and is not something you do alone. She and her colleagues problem-solve together, focusing on equipping the student to progress in their education to give them a better chance in life. Now that is making an impact. I asked her what she did for fun, and she said she enjoys reading. The author Bob Goff has particularly inspired her. Please, meet Mary.

I found Gigi, a volunteer, helping parents get their children signed in for their classroom in Ridge Kids. When there was a lull in new arrivals, we started talking about children. I discovered she doesn't have any kids of her own but selflessly volunteers to help those who do. As I remember back to when I had small children, it was always so nice to know caring adults were looking out for them when I wasn't there.

Gigi is from Dallas originally. She attended Stephen F. Austin State University and pursued a career in real estate right away. She and her husband, Richard, moved to Austin eight years ago after deciding that Austin would be an excellent place to retire. They liked Driftwood and have settled there.

Gigi has three siblings: two of them live in Oklahoma, and one lives in St. Louis. Since they believe in taking care of family, they moved Richard's mom here two years ago, when she was eighty-eight years old, for her to be closer to them. I would be remiss if I did not mention that Gigi also loves dogs. They are the four-legged part of her family. She has three right now: a lab mix, a beagle mix, and a rat terrier. They used to have as many as five at one time—and I thought I was a dog lover!

Professionally, Gigi said she enjoys working with families in transition. I would say buying a house is indeed a significant transition. When she was younger, Gigi worked with a lot of families just getting started, then young career women, then those moving up the ladder. Now she tends to work with retired, empty nesters, as well as those looking for independent or assisted living for loved ones. If this fits your situation, you can read more about her on her website at www.realtyaustin.com/agents/Gigi-McClaskey.

When I asked Gigi about her hobbies, she said she loves to watch golf. She enjoys going to a lot of tournaments because of the great atmosphere, and it is relaxing to be outside. Gigi also enjoys visiting with friends. She feels blessed that they were able to pick a location her friends enjoy visiting and vacationing. Please, meet Gigi.

I went to my hair appointment, and my hairdresser, Cherlyn, introduced me to the owner of her business park, Janie, who has lived in Austin her whole life. She is married and is the eleventh of twelve children. She has four additional half-siblings on her father's side, and they all live in Austin. Janie has longevity in her genes: her mom lived to be ninety-two. I want to know her secret—other than having twelve children!

Janie said she had a delightful childhood. She told me she is just now realizing they weren't rich because she thought they were. Her dad used to make a dish called magic bread made out of two ingredients: flour and gravy. She thought she was lucky to have that because nobody else did; she didn't know it was because they didn't have a lot of food. She said there were not a lot of material things, but somehow, she always thought they were rich. It was terrific having each other.

Only one of her siblings graduated from college. Janie took a few courses but went to work without graduating and was on her own at eighteen. Determined to support herself, she took a job at a convenience store, then worked for a bank for twelve years. After the bank, she worked as an assistant to the office manager for a law firm for six years. She left that job to manage a convenience store because she was not the office type and preferred to be around people of all kinds. She did that for five years before working for Motorola which became Freescale.

Somewhere along the way, Janie became a black belt in martial arts. You would never have guessed this about her if you happened to meet her on the street. She started training with an instructor from Korea then later learned more from her brother; he had joined the military and studied Korean martial arts while serving during the Vietnam War. Janie became so good that she started teaching martial arts after-hours at Motorola. She loved it so much that she taught at the park, in her garage, and eventually in a studio. Her very first studio was in one of the very same buildings she now owns and rents out to others. How that came about is a story of vision, determination, and a lot of something else.

Mr. Nelson Pruitt owned the building originally; Janie had rented her first apartment from him when she was eighteen. She told him that when she got older, she was going to buy one of his buildings. When he was in his seventies, she was renting one of his two buildings because her martial arts business had expanded. When he put the building up for sale, a wealthy investor offered him more than he had initially asked for and was going to pay him cash. Janie called Mr. Pruitt and told him this was her building, and he could not sell it. Mr. Pruitt asked her, "What do you have to offer?"

She said, "I have ten thousand dollars, and I need you to finance the rest for me."

He told her he was going to have to pray about it. He went home, prayed, went to bed, then woke up the next morning and told her, "It's yours, let's do some paperwork." I don't know about you, but I would call that a miracle. He told her, "I like what you have been doing for the community."

Now, let me tell you about her community work. Janie takes in kids from the streets that have been getting into trouble and teaches them martial arts. She has also taught in many after-school programs for the local schools. If you are not familiar with martial arts, for many, it is a way of life. In her programs, Janie teaches children manners, respect for themselves, respect for others, and respect for the property of others. She teaches them about integrity, perseverance, self-control, and the indomitable spirit; she teaches them to give to the less fortunate and visit the elderly. There is an elderly facility right next door to her training facility, and Janie will take the children there (with their parent's permission, of course). The children learn a lot from her because she provides them a learning environment where they know they are listened to and loved.

Though she does not have any children of her own, Janie has a soft spot for them. She said she has "little gardens all over town, and she has to water them; they're just little people, and they want to be heard." That resonated with me because I remember as a little girl wanting someone to "hear me." Janie takes the time to listen. It is no wonder then that she now finds herself teaching the children of adults she once taught as children, and it is not uncommon for her to have students for twenty or more years, even though she does not have contracts.

Janie believes anyone can learn and is willing to work with anyone who wants to increase their knowledge. She said she has worked with people who have disabilities, those in wheelchairs, those who are missing a limb, or who can't talk or hear. Regardless of the disability, she believes she can still teach someone if they are willing.

Janie is a fifth-degree black belt in Taekwondo but also adds a few other arts in her teaching. She has been inducted into the U.S. Martial Arts Hall of fame a couple of times and considers this art a way of life. If you are interested in training in Austin, her school is known as the Ultimate Challenge Martial Arts. You can reach her at jvkarate@aol.com. Although I often hear people lamenting about how "old-fashioned" certain things are, to learn about Janie is one instance when going old school won't hurt you; her martial arts business is mostly referral-based.

I'd say Janie has accomplished a lot. She is a multi-talented businesswoman; she owns the entire business plaza now. Additionally, she is a CBD distributor, which includes tinctures and oils for seizures.

Janie enjoys spending time with her family. She is especially close to four of her sisters and relishes their time spent together. She likes to golf, play tennis, and shoot at a gun range. She is very involved with her church and enjoys living life to the fullest. Janie has developed an appetite for travel; she has been to Puerto Rico, Costa Rica, Colorado, and New York and plans to continue exploring. Before we ended our conversation, Janie had to tell me about the newest little love in her life: her four-year-old goddaughter Brooklyn. Brooklyn has her own room in Janie's home when she comes to visit. Please, meet Janie and Brooklyn.

Lester works at the car dealership where I was getting my car serviced. As he walked past me, I hesitated just a moment before I pushed through and approached him to see if he had a minute to chat. When I told him this was being posted on Facebook, he paused; he was the subject of a post that went viral in 2017 which was then picked up by the news, Rachel Ray, and a few others. I'll tell you about that in a minute, but first let me tell you about Lester, the person.

Lester was born and raised in Austin and is an only child. He is married and has five children, the oldest of whom is in college. He started as a salesman at the dealership he currently works for now but left to join the Navy, where he served for six years; most of that time was on the U.S.S. Enterprise. After the Navy, he was ordained as a pastor. He has pastored in conjunction with working full-time. In addition to Texas and on the sea, Lester has lived in Virginia and D.C. He spends the bulk of his spare time with his family and studying for his Ph.D.

Now, the reason Lester received so much attention two years ago: while he was standing in line behind a teacher, he found out she was buying three cartloads full of school supplies for her students, many of whom she knew could not afford some of the basics. When she got to the cash register, he decided he was going to pay for those supplies and did so before she could refuse. The teacher asked him if she could take his picture. She did, but she did not get his name. Later, this teacher, Sabrina, tried to track him down so she and her school could thank him. She put together a video with his picture in it that went viral until he was located. As of writing this, you can read all about it by looking up, "stranger buys teachers school supplies."

As a result of this publicity, other people found out about it and have taken up the challenge to help teachers. Lester got offers to do several shows, but the one he went on was the Rachel Ray show; they had lined up Yoobi, a school, home, and office supply company that gives back, which provided much-needed school supplies that year for every single child at Francis R. Scobee Middle School! In addition, the Rachel Ray show gave everyone in the audience one hundred dollars with the instructions to find a stranger and pay it forward. The show taped on Lester's birthday. He told me he thought, "What a great way to spend my birthday!"

Lester believes each of us has the opportunity to bless one another. He said that when he freely gives, he finds he has no worries. He then started to talk about Christmas being right around the corner and informed me there is a wealthy man that drives around Austin and goes to the Wal-Marts in the city to pay off layaways for people he doesn't know. He mused, wouldn't it be cool if we did that at Christmas for layaways with toys on it? Please, meet Lester.

I introduced you to Laura in the last chapter. Now, I would like to introduce you to Amy, who hosted Laura's Noonday party. Amy is from Memphis, Tennessee. Talking to Amy reminded me of the wonderful time I spent living in Tennessee. Amy moved to Austin right before she started high school. She attended Texas State for her undergraduate degree in communication disorders followed by a graduate degree from Texas Women's University in Denton in the same field. Naturally, with her background, she became a Speech-Language Pathologist.

Amy began her career working for a private practice in North Austin. She worked in both pediatric and adult cases. It was after she had her first daughter that she decided to do PRN— which means as-needed work. She eventually transitioned into a part-time job until her husband Lance's employment necessitated a move to Dripping Springs. Relocating to Dripping Springs worked out well for her family, as she was able to start working full-time for a school. Besides, there is a daycare facility on campus, making this job the ideal employment opportunity for Amy. "The Sisterhood Across The Globe" rings true (reference from Laura's story.) Now that they have their second daughter, Amy can take both girls to work with her.

Amy also participates in missions with her husband, who is the Director of Missions at Friendship Creekside Fellowship. Together they have been on mission trips to Uganda, Belize, and India. Amy has a heart for missions, which is how she got connected to Laura in the first place. In her spare time, which there isn't much of, she enjoys photography and visiting with family and friends. Please, meet Amy.

I went to a BWIB organizational Christmas party and met Ebonie. Since I went early, I got a chance to see who I already knew and whom I didn't. Ebonie is quite bubbly, and I noticed throughout the evening that she was very generous in spreading her good cheer. After she introduced herself to me, I discovered she works full-time, is the CEO of a non-profit, and assists the BWIB organization as the director of their internship program.

Ebonie is originally from Gary, Indiana and grew up with her brother who is one year younger than her; that's right, the home-town of Michael Jackson and the Jackson 5. She graduated from high school and moved to Indianapolis. Once she decided college wasn't for her, she entered the workforce. Ebonie lived in Indianapolis for thirteen years and held down two jobs: one in healthcare and one in apartment management. When her brother moved to Austin, she decided to move here too in 2011 so she could be closer to him. Ebonie expressed a genuine appreciation for the opportunities that have come her way. Over the past eight years, she and her daughter have planted roots. When she isn't taking care of her home or working, she is busy with Mission Accomplished as the CEO. Her non-profit, Mission Accomplished, focuses on caring for the homeless.

Ebonie is thrilled with her healthcare position because it enables her to connect with the issues people are dealing with regarding mental health and alcohol addiction; she has a passion for this work. You can learn more about her other compassionate efforts at www.mission-accomplished.org. Ebonie puts her money where her mouth is, even taking people into her own home when needed. Regularly she, along with other volunteers, provides a laundry service for the homeless to increase self-esteem and confidence. She will take their clothes, wash, dry, fold them, and then take the clothes back to them. That's a real act of kindness.

I asked Ebonie what inspired her to start her non-profit. She told me she was raised in a church where they always helped individuals, and that there was a homeless shelter right there on-site: that they would routinely do outreach in the community ministering to the homeless out on the streets, meeting them where they were. They went into the prisons as well as nursing homes and children's homes. They were more outside the church than inside the church. "It's in my DNA." When I asked her about her hobbies, she told me she enjoys helping and that, "when I get to see other people's smiles, that makes me smile." And smile, she does. Please, meet Ebonie.

Joel and I ran out to Lowes to grab a few more Christmas lights to finish up a tree outside. While Joel was surveying the available lights, I decided to see if I might meet someone willing to share their story. I noticed a gentleman waiting for his order at the paint counter. I approached him, told him about my challenge, and asked if he would be willing to participate. He hesitated for only a minute, and then he said, "Sure, I think I can do that." His name is David.

David is from Texas City, Texas, a city in Galveston County. He came to Austin when he left home in the early eighties to attend the University of Texas, and he never left. David is one of four children, having an older brother and sister, and one younger brother who has passed away. David has been married for twenty-seven years and has two children. He has a sixteen-year-old and a twenty-three-year-old. His oldest recently graduated from the University of Texas also.

David worked while he went to school for his undergraduate degree in sociology. Upon graduation, he went to work for the Boys and Girls Club of Austin for more than ten years. He then decided to go back to school to earn his MBA in Organizational Learning and Management.

Upon completing his degree, David transferred from the club to the city, working as the Community Liaison Supervisor for the Austin Police Department under Chief Stan Knee. There he focused on community policing, implementing a community policing philosophy where he worked with churches, state institutions, nonprofits and neighborhood associations to keep them abreast of what was going on in the police department. He views his time in this capacity as an excellent opportunity to create community. David left there to become the Executive Director of a private family institution called A Glimmer of Hope Austin.

A Glimmer of Hope Austin was the vision of a couple who had done well in business and who wanted to start investing in nonprofits that work with youth and seniors in Texas. They support innovative programs that improve the lives of youth and senior populations who suffer from exclusion, social injustice, and neglect.

A Glimmer of Hope Austin does not fundraise for operating cost, and 100% of all donations go directly to development projects. They have donated $8.5 million over the years to between 170 and 180 nonprofits. If you are interested in finding out how you can make a difference in the lives of youths, seniors, and people with disabilities, feel free to visit their website at www.aglimmerofhopeaustin.org. David said it is remarkable work.

David enjoys reading, sports, basketball, and fishing: anything outdoors. When I asked him if there was anything else you should know about him, he said, "I thank God for the ability to do any and everything I've been able to do: to guide and allow me to be a blessing to others, that's exciting too! I just go about my day trying to be present, to be a servant." Please, meet David.

8

FINDING JOY

"We must accept finite disappointment,
but we must never lose infinite hope."

—Martin Luther King

It is impossible to be prepared for some of life's twists and turns. The more difficult the circumstance, the more critical it is not to let yourself fall into isolation. Isolation is a dangerous place. It is where your trial can grow into all you can see. Trials come in all shapes and sizes, but hope is strong medicine. I believe that sometimes you must go in search of hope.

I lost my sister when I was twenty-six; she was forty-three. It was the love of family and friends that carried me through that first year until the cloud lifted. One friend said to me that they would be praying when I couldn't. Friends stood in the gap, and the family came together. Later, when I lost my father, again, family and friends came together and provided support; but this time, I also went in search of hope. I realized in the depth of my pain that it was so excruciating because I had loved and been loved so deeply. I was comforted by that thought. Though the pain was there for a while, I was thankful for the father I had been blessed to have had, and for the time I had with him. The cloud of pain and anguish did not last as long as it probably would have had I not found something for which to be thankful.

Everyone grieves differently, and everyone handles life's challenges differently. But after speaking with several who shared about personal loss or trying situations, what stood out to me was they did not try to walk it alone.

I met a fellow extrovert, Devon, at our church lunch. The intent of the lunch was for us to meet and get to know others. Joel and I didn't follow instructions and were sitting with friends (shhh, don't tell the pastor!). Halfway through lunch, Devon showed up at our table. He sat himself down across from me and announced, "I want to get to know y'all." Now, I'm impressed: Devon does follow instructions.

Devon is eighteen years old and fills out every bit of his 6'1, 280-pound frame! In his picture, you can see he easily towers over me. He has a twin brother who weighs 150 pounds; they are *not* identical twins. He also has an older sister. His family is from Wisconsin and moved to Texas in 2009 when his mom was offered a job here. Listening to his story, I admire his mom's courage and determination.

Devon spoke of his journey to his Christian faith: how he had been searching. Eventually, a friend invited him to youth group, and he kept coming because he liked the people. He finally started to go to church, where he heard a sermon series on Jesus Plus Nothing that resonated with him. What impressed me the most about Devon's story was his maturity and self-awareness. Towards the end of our talk, he said, "I'm just mostly thankful because this is how I found my faith."

Devon just graduated from high school. He is looking for a job and hopes to attend one of our outstanding Texas colleges next year. He would like to major in business management. In the future, Devon thinks he might own his own real estate business. He has completed all the coursework for his real estate license but needs to take the exam—a great young man with a vision for his future. Please, meet Devon.

I would like to introduce you to Billie Jo. She is a strong and devoted single parent. She grew up on the coast near Corpus Christi and is the youngest of four children—by fifteen years. I asked her how that was growing up; she said she had a lot of parents.

Billie Jo told me that she once went to a bar when she was seventeen to "play pool." Okay, we'll roll with that. One of her older brothers "happened" to walk into the bar, came over to her and said, "Let's get in the truck," and indicated she could come back later when she was old enough to drink. She also told me her mom was in a ladies' group that would watch out for everyone's children. If she did something, it would get back to her mom five times exaggerated. With all that love going around, she felt like she couldn't get away with anything.

Billie Jo taught special education for eight years and often worked two jobs. As her son got older, she wanted to be more available. She is now working for a small business called Clean

Food Crush, which gives her more flexibility in her schedule; she raved about her great boss. She is also branching out on her own as a virtual assistant focusing on social media platform management, customer support, email support, and the like. If you need help with any of these types of services, you can contact her at pitonyakb@gmail.com

Billie Jo is very proud of her fifteen-year-old son and goes to the gym with him every morning at five a.m.; she describes him as an amazing son who is very structured, positive, and conscientious about his schoolwork.

Billie Jo is very close to her family. She told me another beautiful story of pair matching similar to Sheri's account in Chapter 5. One of Billie Jo's brothers needed a donor, but Billie Jo was not a match. Instead, she donated one of her kidneys to a person she was a match with, and someone in their family donated one of their kidneys for her brother. Game changer! Please, meet Billie Jo.

I met Tommy fifteen minutes before one of our local coffee shops closed. He was drinking a cup of coffee and decompressing after

a long day of work. That is significant because he allowed me into his quiet time; by the end of our conversation, I felt truly honored. You'll understand more in a minute.

Tommy is married, has a seven-year-old daughter, and is originally from Baton Rouge, Louisiana. He and his wife went to high school and college together. They moved to Austin for her job.

Tommy started working in landscaping at fifteen, and at the same time, he started working as a volunteer firefighter in the Explorer Program. He continued firefighting through college. When Tommy came to Austin, he became a paramedic while continuing his work as a landscaper. He went back to school in 2008 and got his Registered Nurse license. Today he works at a large hospital as a registered nurse in the pediatric ICU.

Tommy enjoys fishing, golfing, and biking. He used to enjoy running to get his cardio in, but over time, he has converted more to biking. He usually bikes by himself, except once a year when he does a group ride from Houston to Austin for the MS-150; this is a two-day fundraising event organized by the National Multiple Sclerosis Society. He is hopeful that one day, his wife will join him on the bike or the golf course.

I asked him what interests him about his job as a nurse. He said working with the kids is very rewarding. They often see illnesses specific to children, and it is no fault of the children that they are sick: they are pretty innocent he explained. He also finds it fulfilling that he gets to work with the parents during this challenging time in their lives.

It turns out Tommy still works two jobs: he works full-time as a nurse and does land planning consultation on his days off. Though they are two very different careers, he has a passion for both and wants his daughter to know she can pursue what she finds fulfilling in life and wants to do.

Tommy says he frequents coffee shops because his work commute is only twelve minutes. The coffee shop gives him a chance to take a break from the constant need to think critically regarding those in his care and reset on his way home. He wants to make sure he is mentally and physically present when he arrives home so that he can be his best for his wife and daughter. That is why I felt especially honored that he would pause and take the time to speak with me. But there is still more.

During our conversation, I found out that heroism is in Tommy's blood: his father was fire chief. Tommy was born the middle child of three sons. His older brother, Chris, was also a firefighter and a reserve police officer. I was sad to hear Chris was killed in the line of duty. Tommy told me they each felt proud to serve.

I came home and read about his brother, Chris, on the internet. I sent Tommy a message telling him that he and his brother are heroes. I am humbled to have had the opportunity to sit at his table today, in a coffee shop, and hear his story. Please, meet Tommy.

My friend, Drucilla, who is involved with the prison ministries I told you about in the last chapter, introduced me to Vicky. Vicky's story is a story of hope after an incredible loss. We sat and visited for three hours. We laughed, I cried, then we laughed some more. Vicky's dream was to grow up, get married, become a mom, and stay home to raise her children. By listening to her story, I can tell that she is an awesome mom and has loved her family well. Her children's names are Alicia, Michael, and Brent.

Vicky is also very close to her parents and her two sisters. They see each other regularly and make a point to tell one another they love each other often. Vicky values her friendships and even has a close friend from the second grade. I tell you this because her family and friends have been her support system throughout her life. Her story is a demonstration of how faith, family, friends, and being transparent when life gets hard can bring about restoration.

Twenty-one years ago, Vicky and her husband lost their daughter, Alicia, in a tragic car crash. It was a freak accident the police thought was probably due to the sun. Alicia and two of her friends were in the car when they had a collision with an eighteen-wheeler: they were killed instantly.

Alicia was eighteen, and just about to begin her senior year in high school. Speaking of her daughter, Vicky said she was beautiful and loved being with her family and friends. She was on the drill team and played in the band. Texans take these just as seriously as they take their football. Alicia knew she was loved because her family told her so quite often.

Vicky also shared that when Alicia was a baby, she worked for her parents in one of their bakeries. Her husband and father knew she wanted to be home with the kids, but they also knew she would never dream of quitting on her parents, so they made a plan. Her dad asked her to go with him to deliver a birthday cake one day. Vicky thought that was odd, but she went anyway. On the way to the delivery address, her father fired her!

Okay, here is just one example where Vicky had me going from tears to laughter. After Alicia's passing, Vicky had to keep going. But she did not try to walk that path alone, not that her family and friends would have let her anyway. They surrounded her with love. She said they would not let her out of their sight for a long while. Understandable, this type of tragedy affects everyone. Vicky also got support through a Facebook group called Grieving Moms Forever. It is specifically for mothers grieving the loss of their child. If you or someone you know would find this group helpful, as of the writing this book, you can find this group at www.facebook.com/grievingmomsforever. Vicky also talked to a grieving specialist and took classes on grief, which she thought were helpful.

Vicky's husband, and her fourteen-year-old son, Michael, naturally had much difficulty dealing with their grief. Everyone handles this type of pain differently. Unfortunately, Vicky's marriage did not survive.

Vicky told me a funny story about Michael when he was sixteen. He called her from his teacher's classroom to ask her to bake cookies—for the next day—for his entire class. She asked him what kind, and with her on the phone, he promptly turned around and asked the room full of students (no pressure there). They voted for chocolate chip cookies and peanut butter cookies. Needless to say, Vicky was baking very late that night. She said she tried to get sympathy from her mom for the short notice, but it didn't work; it was payback because she and each of her sisters had done the very same thing to their mom when they were growing up. Again, she had me laughing; we laughed a lot.

In case you haven't figured it out, Vicky enjoys baking and cooking. She also loves to scrapbook. When I asked her if she had other hobbies, she told me she likes to make homemade cards with her mom and enjoys shopping at Hobby Lobby and Michaels.

Vicky later married David whom she met at church. David had a son named Brent, who was already a young adult. Vicky treated him like she did her biological children. Not long after she and David married, Brent lovingly began calling her Mom and would often introduce her to others that way. Vicky knew of Brent through church and had been praying for him long before she had met David: Brent had battled cancer twice. As it happened, after she became his mom, the disease came back. Brent lived to be twenty-six. David told her she was a compassionate caregiver to Brent, and she loves that she got to love Brent as a son.

Vicky has lost two children. I cannot begin to fathom the depths of her heartache. I asked her what she would want others to take away from her story. Here is what she said: There is still life after loss. It's not the same, but there can be happiness again. She said people have asked her what to say or not say to someone who has had a similar experience. Her advice is, "Don't tell a person that their loved one is in a better place. It's one thing if it is a grandparent, but not when it's your child. They don't want to hear that at that time. If you don't know what to say, just hug them. That's it."

Vicky told me the other thing people should not say is, "I know how you feel; I lost my Mom or Dad." Vicky says don't say that because, no, you don't know how they feel.

As I have said, people grieve differently, but for the most part, people who've lost a child want to hear their kid's name; they want to talk about their child, but people are afraid to ask. From her support groups, she learned that parents don't like the fact that other people act like their child was never here. She also shared that sometimes families won't even talk about it to you. Fortunately, Vicky's family and friends were not like that. They would speak about Alicia and sometimes share stories that Vicky had never heard. This was helpful. She said friends should always reach out.

Talking to Vicky allowed me to feel the gamut of emotions. She has such strength and is living life to the fullest with love, all the while spreading hope and joy. Please, meet Vicky.

I went to the co-working space, the Sententia Vera Cultural Hub, to get a change of pace. There I met seventy-three-year-old Carol. I was immediately struck by her humility and the warm smile that made her eyes twinkle. Her story is one of love, prosperity, trial, and perseverance.

Carol is originally from Minnesota and taught German and government before she married her husband, Jamie, who was from San Angelo, Texas. She met him soon after she graduated from college when he had come to Minnesota for a job. She loved his Texan accent, which she referred to as "foreign." They met in the bar at the celebration of a hotel opening. Since he was from a Southern Baptist family, when they told the story of how they met, they would have to leave the bar part out. They had three children together and were successful in blending their different backgrounds and forging a happy life together.

Carol's family was very politically involved. Her uncle was Harold Stassen, the twenty-fifth governor of Minnesota. His nickname was The Boy Wonder. Her mother worked, voluntarily, as his secretary. Carol has pictures of herself sitting in a few of his large meetings.

Interestingly enough, her uncle was one of the writers of the United Nation's Charter. He had been tapped by FDR to go to the first UN pre-meetings. Before that, he had served as the administrative assistant to Admiral Halsey. In this role, he designed strategy which enabled each of the admiral's trusted advisors to see where their respective interests were being met in the planning of one of the last battles of the Pacific.

Following in her uncle's footsteps, Carol also ran for public office as a state representative from her hometown before moving to Texas. When I asked her about this experience, she said it was very eye-opening and taught her how complicated it was to try to represent multiple interests while staying true to your personal beliefs.

Through some handsome returns on wise investments, she and her husband, Jamie, were able to buy the ranch he always wanted. They settled in Menard, Texas. As she had grown up poor, Carol was able to fulfill a passion of hers of helping those less fortunate. She found herself wondering, *Am I just supposed to sit here by the river and enjoy this beauty?* She decided it was too beautiful to keep to herself, so they opened up their ranch to those less fortunate by offering it as a retreat. She said it was so beautiful that people often commented that it reminded them of Tuscany. In addition to their retreat, Carol decided to open a restaurant where she could feed and entertain her community. She had that restaurant for ten years and even had some celebrity patrons: the man who published Harry Potter, and the great, great-grandson of the King of Prussia!

Life was good, then tragedy struck. Her husband, Jamie, was killed in an accident on the ranch. It was quite a shock. Carol had a hard time going back to the restaurant and her hospitality endeavors; it did not hold the same meaning it once had. After four years, she decided to leave the ranch and move to Austin to be closer to where two of her three children lived. In the healing process, she found she needed to find herself again, which she did.

Carol looks forward to the future. She is contemplating writing a book about the wonderful stories coming out of a nonprofit organization that her sister runs called Stay Connected. Stay Connected stands beside less fortunate families for the long haul and provides opportunities for the children to make a better way for themselves. Hearing the stories her sister has shared has made her aware her opportunities were much different than what some others have experienced. Talking to Carol was very inspiring. She loves learning and has embraced keeping up with technology; texting with her grandkids has its perks. Please, meet Carol.

I attended a Young Life fundraiser, where I met Joe. We chatted briefly, but there was not much time as the program was starting. Incidentally, I had unknowingly met and visited with his wife, Ashley. I told you her story in Chapter 4. Fast forward a few days, and I run into Joe. He immediately tells me I just interviewed his wife, Ashley! When I heard her name, I knew right away who she was. So now, I want you to meet Joe.

Joe's story highlights the importance of organizations like Young Life and the importance of adults who take the time to sew into a young person's life. Let me give you some context for his story. Joe's father was born in Calabria, Italy. His father was one of eight children whose mother became a single parent when her husband died. At the time, Joe's father was only three. That left the family destitute: nine people living in a two-room shack.

Joe's grandmother was allowed to send one of her eight children to the U.S. for a better life. At the age of nine, Joe's father was sent to live with his uncle in the U.S.

Imagine being nine years old, not speaking any English, sent to live with family members you don't know well, and getting beat up regularly on the way to school because you don't fit in. He didn't feel like he fit in with his uncle's family either and developed a "victim mentality." Unfortunately, Joe's father dropped out of high school, and at the age of sixteen, with the help of an old man he knew, his father started his first pizzeria. Joe said his father was an incredible cook but was horrible with everything else. You now have a backdrop of some of the challenges facing young Joe growing up.

Joe was the oldest of three children. His father started several restaurants, moving the family back and forth from New York to Texas a couple of times, with one move to Oklahoma before ultimately settling back in Texas. His dad worked long hours, often sleeping at the restaurant. Both his mother and father had addiction problems. Joe told me that when he looks back, he knows God had a hand in his survival because his mother often drove drunk. "God just protected us. That's the only explanation." He mentioned that because of growing up that way, he carried a lot of shame.

Joe credits a particular class in high school with freeing him from feeling all alone. It was a class where the students had to be nominated to participate. The course consisted of two days going to an elementary school and volunteering to be like a big brother or big sister. The other three days of the week they would be in a classroom. The administration was mindful of the cliques in the school when choosing participants and selected around twenty kids that ordinarily would not have talked to each other. There were a few athletes, cheerleaders, band members, drama students, skaters, and stoners all together in one class. Joe explained that his teacher had a way of getting the students to open up about their lives. By the end of that semester, all but one student had shared hard pieces of their lives: some shared about attempted suicide, others shared about abuse.

It was in this class where Joe went from no one knowing about his real-life to him being open about it and no longer feeling shame. He commented on the importance of teachers and that they have access to young people who are going through some tough things. That is also why Young Life is so important to him now. Joe felt compelled—no, privileged—to support this organization; it provides a similar atmosphere to the one his teacher fostered where young adults can find a supportive, encouraging environment to discover they are not alone and that there are adults who care.

Although he faced some troublesome circumstances in his home life, amazingly, Joe was able to find his way onto the campus of Texas A&M. But Joe's challenges were far from over. On the home front, his father, who had been a heavy smoker and drinker, died of cancer at age fifty-three. His brother struggled with addictions. Sadly, his brother was involved in a horrific motorcycle accident while under the influence of drugs and alcohol. His brother survived the crash but suffered a similar spinal cord injury to the one that paralyzed Christopher Reeves. Unable to breathe without an artificial respirator, his brother decided to be taken off of life support. Then six years ago, his mother, also a heavy smoker, passed away from cancer at the age of sixty-three. Again, his explanation for the ability to overcome his circumstances is that God shielded him and made way for a positive path forward.

Following graduation from A&M, Joe worked as a valet and also as a substitute teacher. He enjoyed being a substitute because some of his students were the younger siblings of prior classmates. Four months after graduating, he got his first full-time job recruiting in the telecom space. He later became a sales team lead. However, due to the volatility of the high-tech field and surviving seven rounds of layoffs before his number came up, he decided to get into something more recession-proof. Joe leveraged his college connections to get into the very competitive field of medical device sales, which is what he does today. He said this field is tough to get into if you don't have the right background; if he had not known his friend, he would not have the great career he has today.

Joe met his wife, Ashley, while at Texas A&M. They have two beautiful children. He enjoys cooking and experimenting with different recipes; homemade pizza and Spanish Paella are two of his specialties. He shared with me that for Italians, good food is great, but more importantly, it is the means for bringing people together. That's the part he loves, bringing people together. He especially enjoys when his girls invite friends over, and he gets to cook for them. In addition to cooking, Joe enjoys hunting, traveling, and hiking with his family when they go on vacations. Ashley's dad has a ranch where he hunts deer and hogs with friends. Fun fact: Joe met Tom Cruise while Joe was an extra in the prom scene of the movie Born on the 4th of July. He confided in me that he was taller than Cruise. Please, meet Joe.

I was introduced to Lory by Ria. I noticed Lory's bright smile as she inquired about what I was doing. As we walked over to a quieter area of the store, she shared that Spike Lee had come to Austin several years ago, gathering stories for a project. At that time, she wasn't ready to tell her story, but she was ready now and thanked me for the opportunity.

Lory is originally from Fort Worth, Texas and had settled in Bastrop, Texas with her husband, Rogers. They were avid motorcyclists. In 2008, they were both on his three-month-old bike and traveling with family members to pay their respects to his mother, who had passed away that same day the year prior. Rogers' bike malfunctioned, and Lory was thrown off the bike and into the median. Thankfully, everybody stopped without hitting her. Her husband, Rogers, did not survive the crash. Lory was airlifted to Breckenridge. She had broken most of the bones in her body and was in a coma for three months. Family members tried to prepare her mother and told her that Lory probably would never walk again. But, Lory is a modern-day miracle: she has made an almost complete recovery.

Lory credits an outstanding nurse with actually getting her to start walking. After coming out of the hospital, she went to live in Michigan. She chose Michigan because a good friend invited her to come up, and she needed a change of scenery with a different environment. Since she was well known in her community, it was difficult to hear so many well-meaning friends and associates say, "Lory, I'm so sorry." In Michigan, she also had the loving support of members from the Welcome Missionary Baptist Church she attended. She spent a year there and was well cared for; but folks, there is a lot of snow in Michigan. Lory found herself missing home, so after a year, she returned to Texas. Still, it took her five years to come to terms with what happened.

Looking back, Lory says God never let her fall; she still feels Rogers' presence—his love guiding her. She counts her blessings that she has known a lot of love. Rogers was her best friend. "And when your best friend is the person that you love, you can't even describe it. It's the best thing in the world. And I know I'm going to be okay." Though it has been a challenge, she believes life goes on, and you can't be sad all the time. She told me she has her moments, but Rogers is always with her in her heart, and that gives her peace.

People encouraged her to sue the motorcycle company, but to her, it doesn't matter; the money would never be enough to make up for what she lost, and she would waste precious time in the process. "Unforeseen things happen. It's what you make out of it." She told me it has made her stronger, and she can be there for people who have gone through similar things if they need to talk. She knows Rogers would want her to keep moving forward.

Lory loves spending time with her mother, sister, brother, niece, and a brand-new nephew. Her niece, who is twenty-four, is like the daughter she never had. She said it's super special that her niece gets to enjoy a brand-new brother at twenty-four.

When asked what she enjoys doing when she's not working, Lory stated that she doesn't ride motorcycles anymore, though she misses it tremendously. Instead, she has turned her attention to doing wedding florals, which she absolutely loves. Horseback riding and traveling are also high on the list of things she enjoys. Please, meet Lory.

I needed to get gift bags, so I stopped by the General Dollar store, and I am glad I did. A very nice young lady named Jessica asked if she could help me. I told her what I was looking for and then asked her if she would also like to help me with my challenge.

She wondered what had sparked my challenge. After I told her the why and what, she happily agreed to participate.

Jessica is from Austin and has a younger brother and sister. She is an overcomer of challenging circumstances. Her mother homeschooled her and her siblings but was ill. As a result, Jessica and her siblings found themselves in public school with little warning of what a drastic change it would be from what they knew. Jessica was sixteen at the time. She and her siblings dug their feet in and figured out how to succeed in this new environment. With sheer determination and hard work, they all graduated from high school with flying colors. Jessica is pretty proud of all they have accomplished.

Jessica was able to help take care of her mother with love when she was passing; yet, for someone so young, that was a lot to go through. There was a lot of confusion, and she had questions: how come her mother couldn't stay around; why wouldn't her mother be there when she got married? It was during this time of trial in her life when Jessica started to see some light and God's hand in her life. She said, "But learning to let go and to love, to be patient and forgive, I think has really opened up doors for me."

Her dad encouraged her even though he didn't have answers to her questions. He told her that someday she would meet people who would need to hear her story, and she would be able to help them because of her experiences. When she spoke about her siblings and herself, she explained that their struggles growing up played a significant role in their growth and development; they are all strong but compassionate and have understanding hearts towards others. When they run into a person who is grumpy or rude, they see this as an opportunity to be patient and caring because they don't know the person's backstory.

After high school, Jessica went to Austin Community College (ACC) part-time and worked part-time, then did both full-time. Once she completed the basics at ACC, she began exploring photography opportunities while rapidly advancing her career in retail. In just three short years, Jessica became the store manager for almost two hundred people. She believes in helping her staff learn new things and encourages them to teach others coming behind them. Right now, her primary focus is on overseeing store operations, but she still plans to earn a four-year degree when the time is right. Jessica is thankful she has a job and says there was a lot to learn, but it has been an enjoyable and rewarding journey. As far as her photography, she has done work for Circuit of the Americas and Ballet Austin. She enjoys family, wedding, engagement, and event photography.

Jessica told me she is excited to become an aunt; her sister is expecting and has already given her a t-shirt that says, "Best Aunt Ever." Jessica enjoys trying new restaurants or cooking new dishes with family and friends. She particularly enjoys reading adventure or leadership books and thinks she has benefitted greatly from some of John C. Maxwell's (a number one New York Times bestselling author, speaker, and coach) writings. Jessica has a strong faith in God and says, "He does what He says. He says, 'I will turn everything around for your good,' and I believe that, and I see that now; God loved on me in my times of need." Please, meet Jessica.

I went shopping to buy a Christmas present and ran into a friend of mine, David. He was in the bookstore with his cousin, Trevor.

Trevor had just moved to Austin, and already he will be moving again. He is originally from Snyder, Texas but has lived a lot of places as a result of his father's work as a petroleum engineer. Let's start with Venezuela during the coup of April 2002. After Venezuela, Trevor lived in Colorado for a year. Next, the family was off to Muscat, Oman in the Middle East. Trevor loved it there and remembered going to a great school and having a lot of close friends. He reminisced that his father loved to fish there; that you could go deep-sea fishing and still see the coast because the coastal plate would drop off abruptly, close to the beach.

One particular excursion he recalled in Oman was caravanning with eight families through desert terrain using land cruiser type vehicles. One of the things they saw was, "like a mountainside where the entire thing was fossilized marine life." He explained that the whole area used to be underwater, way, way, way back when. "It was just incredible and beautiful to see; it was also really strange because there was nothing there and so hot in the day, like a hundred twenty degrees, then it would drop to forty degrees at night."

From Oman, his parents, he, and his brother moved back to Austin, which was a big culture shock to Trevor. He indicated it was harder to come back to the U.S. than it was to leave because he didn't know the pop culture or sports, which is so ingrained in what everybody does in America. The next family move—to Katy, Texas—was easier. Surprisingly, he was able to reconnect with friends he had known previously in Venezuela and Oman.

Upon returning to the United States while Trevor was in high school, his father was diagnosed with cancer. Trevor told me "they" cured it, then on a routine scan one year later, "they" found it again. His father died two weeks later. Understandably, this was tough for young Trevor to process, and he shut himself off from the world.

Trevor said three things helped him a great deal in processing his grief. The first thing was that his friends allowed him to take life at his own pace but gently encouraged him to do things he once enjoyed; it didn't make the grief go away, but it made him maintain his social connections. Second, he participated in a grief counseling group at his school. Third, he also saw a grief counselor outside of school, which was a tremendous help. Trevor shared that this is what worked for him; everyone processes grief differently, but he hopes this may be of help to someone else.

Trevor attended the University of Houston. He had planned to become an engineer like his father and two of his uncles until physics caused a problem. He described it as, "My life plan up to that point crashed and derailed." Being open-minded, he moved forward and earned an undergraduate degree in econometrics, followed by a master's degree in applied economics. By this time, he had come to think of Houston as home and admitted he became pretty stubborn about getting a job there. Then Hurricane Harvey hit, and that didn't happen. In time, Trevor had to shift his perspective once more and started applying elsewhere, which brings me to why he is moving yet again. He recently landed a great job as an economist! Even though he will be moving again, he is excited about this opportunity. Things are looking up.

Trevor enjoys cooking and rock climbing. The rock climbing is something he has recently learned how to do and finds it actively challenging. "You have to think about what you're doing and be strong enough to do it." In spite of the challenges behind, he has a very bright future ahead of him. Please, meet Trevor.

I passed by Winner Winner Rotisserie and Fine Foods on my way to a children's play place a friend had mentioned to me. Winner Winner is a diner on Hwy-290 that is inside of a train car. I have been passing by this for at least a year and have always wondered about it. I decided to stop in today, and when I did, I met Jessi, an employee there.

Jessi was born in Austin, then moved to Blanco and Dripping Springs while in middle school and high school and now resides in Austin once again. Jessi told me she grew up impoverished. Her mom left her husband of six years when Jessi was ten. They didn't have any place to go, so they lived in a tent for six months in the woods, then a barn storage room in Blanco, Texas, for six months. She and her mom would shower at the local state park where they had a pass. "So we had our own little shower kits, and we'd take them in there. It was pretty wild." I asked her what having that experience taught her. She thought a minute and told me it taught her the value of money for sure and to be humble. It also taught her a lot of survival skills: how to live on very little, and it gave her an appreciation for life.

After high school, Jessi got a job in administration and felt that she had to grow up real fast. At the age of eighteen, she was working in offices while all of her friends were going to college. She felt very old. Eight years later, Jessi was working in the food-service industry and found her true calling. I asked her what made food service so appealing to her. What she loves is serving people good food and seeing the expressions on their faces when they are eating. Though she enjoys cooking, she sees herself more like a front-of-the-house person. "I'm more of the customer service; that's my bag. I love interactions. I love the socialization of it." She also told me she loves that it is fast-paced.

Her twenties were hard, but now she is doing well. She told me she tries not to take things for granted. She is happily married and has a cat named Monster. "I always let cats pick their own names, and he picked that one." She was very light-hearted and said, "He's horrible." We laughed. For fun, Jessi loves to cook with her husband. They spend a lot of time on food prep and enjoy that as well. She also likes playing video games and is good at pool, though she doesn't get to play very often. Jessi told me she is in a great place in her life right now; she finds herself taking things for granted sometimes and has to be mindful that some people don't have anything. We talked a little bit more, and she told me life is hard, but I got the sense from her that she is not one to let life get the best of her. As we continued our conversation, I was encouraged to hear that not only is she doing well, her mom is too. I found myself feeling inspired by this young woman as we sat, and she shared encouraging words of wisdom with me. Please, meet Jessi.

9

MILITARY LIFE

"Bloom where you are planted."

—Bishop of Geneva, Saint Francis de Sales

"Bloom where you're planted," is the call to the military family. When individuals enter the military, they are young (usually late teens to early twenties) and very often single. They come from all different backgrounds, and through a process known as basic training, they are molded into airmen, soldiers, sailors, marines, or coast guard; they are trained to serve. The motto "service before self" becomes ingrained in their thought process.

Somewhere along the line, many get married. The spouse—without the benefit of basic training or belonging to a unit and bereft of family living close by—is expected to mold into the military way of life: bloom where you're planted. They are adjusting to a new life apart from family or their pre-existing support system. If they are lucky, the military unit may have something in place for the spouses to bond. Then perhaps there are children involved. The children also are expected to pick up and move with each new assignment with their military parent or stay put while the military parent leaves for an assignment. If the latter is the case, the spouse then holds the fort down and does the job of two. What is expected of the children? "Bloom where you're planted."

Being a military spouse with now-grown children myself, I realize that it isn't until much later that the sacrifices of the family are understood more fully. When the military member separates from the service, the whole family abruptly loses its tribe. The military member answers the call, as does the entire family. The following stories are a snapshot of people connected to the military who are expected to pick up and move with each assignment and make life work.

I would like to introduce you to Angela. I met her at a Symposium that was held at the George Washington Carver Museum in Austin. She is an Army veteran of twenty-five years, a wife, mother of three, and a grandmother of two. Currently, she works for the Veterans Administration, is an Ambit Energy consultant, and is the founder of Numbers Evolution, which is a mobile math tutor business; she sure is juggling multiple roles.

Angela has lived in Austin the past three-and-a-half years and loves to travel. She makes it a point to go somewhere new every year. She has lived all over the world: Democratic Republic of Congo, Namibia, Australia, New Zealand, France, Switzerland, Japan, Canada, Greenland, Jamaica, Virgin Islands, Mexico and, of course, the United States. Stateside, her military travels have also provided opportunities for her to have lived in Texas, Louisiana, South Carolina, New York, Missouri, California, Wisconsin, Virginia, Alabama, Hawaii, and Arizona. Additionally, she has visited almost all of the other fifty states. I would say she is very well-traveled, wouldn't you?

At the VA, Angela helps soldiers adjust back to their families after they return or even before they go downrange; she performs a crucial role for our active-duty military. Angela is also the kind of person who volunteers to take on additional functions when she joins an organization. (She didn't tell me that, I witnessed it myself.) She looks for where she can plug-in and help out. You will also find her showing up to support her friends in their various endeavors.

I asked her how she got involved with being a mobile math tutor. Angela said the son of someone she knew was struggling with math, and she offered to help because she knew math was one of her strengths. When the mother offered to pay for her help, she thought, wow, this is a perfect match. She was able to merge helping others, her love of math, and earning an income all into one. Angela says her ideal student is kindergarten through sixth grade. If your child needs a math tutor in the Austin area, why not get in touch with her? You can contact her at www.numbersevolution.com. Please, meet Angela.

You never know who you will meet or where. Driving home from a trip Joel and I took to Dallas, we stopped at an Exxon gas station. A gentleman dressed in Elvis attire was setting up shop.

His name is Carl. He began impersonating Elvis when he was in the Army. I started reading his signs: one read "FREE HUGS;" another said "Disabled Veteran;" a third sign read "Singing and Photos for Tips;" and a fourth said "CD's for $10." Carl had lots of signs!

I didn't get the story I expected. Carl was medically retired from the Army: he entered the military when he was seventeen and served our nation for ten years. He then continued to serve in the police department and retired from that after twenty-four years. Now at sixty years old, Carl said he sings and takes pictures to kill time and to meet people. He didn't start with it in mind, but people tell him this is a ministry. During our conversation, Carl made some comments that resonated with me. He said just saying "Hi" can change someone's life. He also said that he enjoys making people happy because "what else is there?" He believes he gets back much more than he gives, and Carl said he'd be lost without this traveling show.

He once saw a guy holding a sign up in a race that said, "Free Hugs." He thought that was awesome and something he could do. He thinks a smile and a hug makes the world go around. I am thinking how wonderful it is that the original sign holder, with his simple act of kindness, inspired Carl to share some, as well. Of course, I got my hug; that's making me smile right now as I write this.

Carl said he sings because music speaks to everyone. "Everyone has a song." He wants people to walk away from him, having heard a song that helps them have a good day. He is passionate about singing. He said his music and interacting with others helps him and uplifts his spirits. "When you think you have it bad, you never know what's going on with someone else. Other people are struggling. What're a few minutes of your time? Listening to their problems makes yours seem small. "

When I asked him if he wanted to share anything else, he said, "People are people. We have to get over this bickering and fighting. We need to speak as a nation. Let's love each other and stop this hate." As Carl and I were about to take a selfie, Joel offered to take the photo for us. While taking the picture, Joel asked Carl if he had served (Joel had not heard our conversation) and then thanked him for his service. Carl then asked Joel if he had served, and thanked Joel for his service accompanied with a salute. Joel returned the salute. At that moment, I saw two strangers connect over a smile, a shared experience, and words of appreciation. It was heartwarming to observe. Please, meet Carl who is sharing with you his smile and Elvis pose.

I met a very affable young man named John at the gym. I have seen him several times because he works there. He is twenty-six, which is about the same age as my older son at the writing of this.

It turns out John is a military brat—but Marine, not Air Force like my family. His father is a retired colonel. Since his dad served for twenty-four years, John moved around a lot in the southeast. He has lived in North Carolina, Florida, Alabama, Texas, Georgia, and Virginia. I asked him how that was for him, and he said it was good; he got to see a lot of different cultures moving from state to state.

John said he went to two high schools, but that wasn't bad because he was able to spend two years in each school and made good friendships at each. He plans to join the Air Force within the next three months, finish up his political science degree, then apply for a spot in Officer Training School (OTS).

John would like to make the Air Force his career. He said he thinks the discipline and structure of the military will be good for him. He hopes to be selected for Para Rescue, the Tactical Air Control Party (TACP) where he would call in close air support or become a combat controller, which is a member of the Air Force Special Operations career field.

John has a younger brother who is a Marine officer, an older sister, and a younger sister. His hobbies include working out, watching football, and playing rugby. His philosophy is to take each day as it comes and enjoy life. After our initial meeting, John and I had several conversations regarding the specialized physical testing required for the programs he was interested in and his progress on them before he went off to boot camp. Please, meet John.

I encountered another person who holds a black belt in martial arts. I met Lance and Mary at the same Young Life fundraiser, where I met Joe from Chapter 8. We both know the same great couple, Jeff and Sheji, who had sponsored our table. I happened to be seated next to Lance.

Lance and Mary have been married for twenty-eight years and have four sons. Let me start with Lance's story first. He grew up in Middleton, Texas. After high school, he spent a little bit of time in college before he decided to join the Marine Corps in which he served for four years.

During his time in the Marines, Lance worked on F-4 Phantoms. He was responsible for maintaining all of the systems for the pilots to communicate, the navigation system, and the electronic countermeasures equipment. When the U.S. shot down Gaddafi's MiGs, he was on the other carrier that was in the Gulf of Sidra at that time. He said there was a lot of firepower on the Navy carrier from which the F-4s launched.

Also, while in the Marines, Lance got married and had two sons. When he got out of the Marines, he went back to school and got a degree in Electrical Engineering. He got a job and moved his family to Corpus Christi. Then life happened, and he got divorced. A couple of years later, he met and married Mary.

Lance has a passion for Karate and has done that most of his life. He is one of Chuck Norris' black belts! Yes, my friends, he has trained with Chuck Norris, earned his black belt under the Chuck Norris system and even has a picture of the two of them hanging in his home. At one point in time, Lance owned a martial arts studio. When he moved, he had to give it up. I'm telling you, you simply never know who folks are and what they know unless you ask. I wouldn't go picking a fight with people I don't know, that's for sure.

Now I'll tell you about his bride, Mary.

Mary grew up in Corpus Christi. She has two brothers and four sons: Lance's two sons and two sons she shares with Lance. There is an eighteen-year difference between the oldest and youngest. Mary said she was surrounded by men until recently when the adoption for their granddaughter was finalized.

Let me tell you a little about her childhood. When Mary started school, she did not speak English, which surprised everyone because she had blue eyes and blond hair. However, she said her parents are from Mexico. Mary grew up Catholic. She received an accounting degree from the University of Texas; while in college, she converted to the Protestant faith and was baptized on New Year's Eve.

Mary moved back to Corpus Christi after college and went to work for Central Power & Light, where she met Lance. She said he came over to her and asked her out; she was not expecting that. They had a short courtship—only a few months—before he asked her to marry him.

Mary is one sharp cookie; she keeps getting job offers she can't refuse. She was offered a job in Austin shortly after her engagement. The company wanted to hire her, so when she told them about her fiancé, and they found out his background, they offered him a job too. Mary and Lance accepted the jobs and moved to Austin. They lived here for eleven years then moved to The Woodlands, Texas. They were only there for nine months (Lance had worked for a little-known company—Enron—right before they went bankrupt). They then moved to Flower Mound, Texas.

After the move, for the first time, Mary became a stay-at-home mom, but she wanted to work part-time. She told me she prayed about this and three days later, a friend of hers who was doing accounting for a church called her up and told her she was quitting her job. Additionally, her friend said to her that she thought Mary was the right person to take over for her. By that time, Mary had her CPA. She was hired by that church to be the finance director. She worked twenty hours a week and from home to boot. For her, this was answered prayer. She worked there for fifteen years.

Last year they moved back to Austin. Their two oldest sons live here, and so does their first grandchild. I would make the same decision. At this point, Mary thought she was retired and told me she prayed again about what she should do next. Then, she received two phone calls that were both job offers on the same day: she had not applied for either position. Having worked with many people in career transition, I know that is pretty miraculous!

Mary said she now works full-time, from home, doing accounting services for non-profits. She enjoys reading, walking, and exploring. Life is good. Please, meet Lance and Mary.

Joel needed to rent another car for business travel and asked me if I would drop him off at the car rental place. I wasn't even going on the trip this time, but I obliged. I was just about to drive off when I thought, *hey, there might be a different person working here today.* Lucky for me, there was, and I got the chance to meet him. His name is Eric.

Before I approached him, I noticed Eric had a professional, friendly, and easy-going personality, which is great, considering he is working with customers every day. He is from Houston and has an older brother and two older stepsisters. His family moved to Wimberley when he was in high school. After high school, Eric went into the Air Force. While in the Air Force, he was able to expand his range of interests and knowledge and learn about a new culture in South Korea. He commented that everyone was respectful and that he had a lot of fun. Even though there was some picketing about the US military presence, the majority of the people were welcoming.

After the Air Force, Eric went back to school. He graduated from Texas State with a degree in Business Marketing. A couple of years later, he found his way to his current job with Enterprise. He is married and has two children, ages four years and six months. When I asked him about his hobbies, Eric told me he enjoys cave diving with his four-year-old son and hanging out at the beach with the entire family.

Eric shared that he and his wife are focusing on how to be better parents. They are feeling a profound responsibility for impacting the next generation, as these children will become the leaders of our country. Eric specifically told me he has a newfound respect for teachers now that he and his wife are just starting on their journey of preparing their children to enter the education system. Like most new parents, they feel challenged at times but are determined to do their best. I remember those days: feeling ill-equipped for the colossal task at hand of raising children. As he talked about his family, I could tell he was energized and committed to being a good father and husband. Please, meet Eric.

My friend Sheji introduced me to Shannon. I had stopped by a coffee shop, and the two of them were talking about work. They both are the leaders overseeing the women's ministry at their respective church campuses. I mention that up-front because most of what Shannon shared with me has a lot to do with multiple moves and her faith journey. Here is her story.

Shannon is originally from Alexandria, Virginia. She attended Mary Washington College and studied business. Since she had been doing administrative work in a doctor's office since she was fifteen, she saw how a small business ran. She met her husband, Ned, while she was in college. Ned is younger than she is, so he still had a couple of years to go after she graduated. Right after college, Shannon took a job that she didn't enjoy that also had a long commute. She quickly found a better position at a company that contracted out facilities management. Shannon had never worked in that area before and loved the challenge. She worked there for three years, learning a lot about business and a little about herself before later working for the World Bank in D.C. All the while, she was dating Ned; he was going through ROTC. Ned went into the Marines right after college. After he graduated, they were married, and he got orders to California.

Married less than two months, they packed their bags, left all family, and headed to 29 Palms in California. Soon after arriving in California, Shannon was on her own because Ned had to go into the field. Having so much free time, Shannon found a job doing administrative work in a school as an office fill-in. It was a confusing time for her. Ned was off doing his duty; she had left her job, family, and friends. Such is the life of a military spouse. Ned was home for the first six months after the birth of their first child, Jack, but was deployed for the next six months. The next assignment was in Washington, D.C.

No sooner had they settled in D.C. than Ned was called back to his old unit. He had trained with them, and they needed him to deploy with them to Iraq. Shannon was expecting their second child at the time. Before he left, he and Shannon had the hard conversations about what would Shannon do if he did not make it back, like what she would name their baby and how she would live. They decided Shannon, Jack, and Elie (their soon-to-be newest addition) would live with Ned's parents for four months. Shannon's family lived only three miles away. Eventually, they settled in at Bolling, Air Force Base which is across the bridge in D.C. Thankfully, Ned did make it back, but he missed the February birth of Elie and did not return until May. When he came back from this deployment, Ned finished out his commitment, and they re-evaluated their lives. They decided it was time to leave the military way of life and become civilians.

Transition out of the military can be hard: not only on the military member but on the family as a whole. For many, it is the life they have known most of their adult lives; that was true for Ned and Shannon—they both lost their tribe and their identity. They were no longer Ned the Marine and Shannon, the wife of a Marine. They were simply Ned and Shannon. This transition did not go well for their family, but Ned did find work in sales in New York, and the family settled there. His employers were people who were following Jesus, and they came into Shannon's life at a crucial juncture. Around this time, Shannon had their third child, Joe. Then due to a downturn in the economy around 2008, there was another job change and a move to Pennsylvania. Significant life changes often produce stress.

With a new job, new surroundings, and after numerous attempts to get on the same page with Ned, Shannon began considering her future options. She was desperate and asked the Lord for freedom from her marriage. She was struggling with control—controlling the situation and who she wanted Ned to be. What came to Shannon in prayer was, "He's mine. I will decide. You just need to worry about yourself"—meaning let go of control.

When Ned came to the realization his marriage was in real trouble, he too began searching for options to get back on the same page. Ned's faith began to grow. Shannon's did too, but real life is not that easy. They hit another impasse.

In his search, Ned stumbled across the book Beyond Anger by Thomas Harbin. The back cover read, "At my tenth wedding anniversary, my wife took me aside and said, 'If the next ten years are anything like the last ten years, I'm out of here because I'm tired of walking on eggshells around you.'" When Ned read that, it sounded eerily close to words Shannon had spoken to him. Ned read the book; for the first time, he began to address the anger that was going on inside. He started to get plugged into the men's group at his church in Pennsylvania, and he also studied the book of John in the Bible. Things began to change. They made one more move to Austin for a job and started attending Austin Ridge.

Staying on the same page has not always been easy, but that's the case for any long-term relationship. Today, Shannon can say with a smile they have a good relationship, and their journey together has been incredible. She is excited about the growth in her spiritual walk over the past twelve years and can see how God's hand has been with them. She says she is learning to trust God more and more, not only with her marriage but also with her children. She has a passion for helping equip other women in their faith journey. Please, meet Shannon.

I was on my way to the gym when I made a detour by Dunkin' Donuts. Wait a minute; it's not what you think: I stopped by there to do research. I was preparing for a presentation I was to give to a group of entrepreneurs on personal branding, and I wanted to check out the feel of their store. While I was there, I met three very kind and generous people. As I explained my challenge, one young lady, in particular, was very enthusiastic. I will tell you about her now.

She introduced herself as Ari, but that's short for Ariana. Ari was born and raised right here in Austin, and she has a brother four years older than she is. She graduated high school early, then enlisted in the U.S. Navy. She attended boot camp at The Great Lakes Naval Training Center, located on the western shore of Lake Michigan, near Chicago. While training, she was injured. This unfortunate sequence of events cut her Navy career short.

After leaving the Navy, Ari tried college but discovered it was not the right time in her life yet. She plans to return and study advertising so she can help advertise her family's tax business. Ari enjoys spending time with her family: a rather large extended family I might add.

Ari loves people. She wants folks to know there are still good people out there. Her other loves are English, writing, working, and staying busy. Please, meet Ari.

Joel and I went to a Christmas open house that our friends Charlie and Georgia hosted in the neighborhood, and I met Maureen. She goes by "Renie" for short. Renie is from northern Kentucky and has one sister. She attended Kentucky College, and while there she met her husband. After college, he was called to be a minister and went to seminary in Louisville, Kentucky for three years. They have four children: three girls and one boy.

For twelve years, Renie worked alongside her husband in northern Kentucky and Illinois leading Sunday school, singing in the choir, and working with the Women's Missionary Union. When her husband was called into the military as a chaplain, their way of life changed dramatically. They moved nine times in ten years. Their first duty station was Ft. Leonard Wood in Montana. During his twenty-seven year career, they lived all over the world: Hawaii, Germany, Vietnam, Korea, and all over the U.S. Renie said one of the best compliments she got was from one of her daughters who said, "Mom always made it a home wherever we were."

Renie completed her bachelor's and master's in counseling and became a counselor working mostly with military families in the area of parenting and other family issues. (She says that military spouses are some of the most remarkable people.) Later, she was on the staff of three different churches throughout Texas and Illinois as a family life educator, which she thoroughly enjoyed. After the military, her husband became the Head of Pastor Care at Baptist Memorial Hospital in San Antonio. They retired to a ranch in Texas.

Renie says she has a great family and is very proud of her children. She is eighty-five, and her husband is eighty-four. Renie believes the constant moves and all the activities they've been involved in have kept them young at heart. They've been blessed with excellent health and great friends. She has four grandchildren and four great-grandchildren. She enjoys doing watercolor paintings and has won many awards, including Best of Show and still participates in shows every year. Renie says, "Life is good and worth living." Please, meet Renie.

10

How Did They Meet?

"The course of true love never did run smooth."

—William Shakespeare

I am not going to claim to be an expert on true love for everyone, but I have been married for thirty years at the writing of this book. I have learned a few things along the way, and I can say that I am happily married. The real question is not how long someone has been married, but do they love each other and are they happily married. Most people describe love as a feeling, but feelings are deceptive. Love is much more than that. Love is an action verb.

The best advice I ever got was that to stay happily married, view marriage like a bank; think of it as a love bank if you will. Before a couple marries, they often make many deposits. Now and again, a withdrawal is made, but usually not at the same rate as the deposits. Somewhere after the marriage, the equation often becomes imbalanced because one or both of the partners start assuming marriage is for life. They start making more withdrawals than deposits, and the union can quickly become bankrupt. To stay married is a daily choice. To love is another daily choice. To have a happy marriage, each part of the couple chooses to make more deposits than withdrawals.

I was introduced to an engaging couple, Craig and Regan, at a mutual friend's four-year-old birthday party. Craig and Regan met each other on eHarmony: a true story. As of writing this, they have been married for nine years! Craig and Regan have two sons, ages five and eight.

Craig is in real estate and owns his own company. Before getting into real estate, Craig was a wrestler and a former professional baseball pitcher. He rose the fastest through the Colorado Rockies' Farm team, and he once threw a 100-mph ball until he injured his elbow and needed surgery; life can throw you a couple of curveballs. Indirectly through that experience, he met the love of his life, Regan.

Regan and I hit it off right away. She has a very vibrant personality. Well, they both do, but I'll focus on Regan for now. The spelling of Regan's name comes from the story of King Lear as well as the movie The Exorcist. Regan says she is a military brat because her father served in the Air Force; when he would move, so would the family. She is officially a Texan because she was born in San Antonio ten days before her family moved to another new assignment. My youngest son, Dillon, is a military brat from Texas, too. He was born in that very same hospital.

Regan's dad decided to get out of the military after twenty years because it was getting harder to move the family once his girls were getting older. I can totally understand that decision from personal experience. Regan said her mom made every move seem like an adventure, but it was harder on her sister, who was four years older.

Regan and her sister both attended Baylor University, and both ended up in Austin. Now, her parents live here too. Regan is a director in Mary Kay and has supported herself with Mary

Kay her entire adult life—even before meeting Craig. Though she sells lipstick, Regan considers herself more of a business coach. She says she loves what she does and that it is so much more than makeup. She feels she gets to invest in the lives of her team and her clients while being able to adjust her schedule to her family's needs. Please, meet Craig and Regan.

I finally got to meet Scott after hearing such great things about him for more than a year. He recently married one of my longest and dearest friends, Lisa. I had a hunch that I would be a fan of his from the very first time Lisa mentioned him because he makes her happy! And after Joel and I spent a weekend with them, I was a fan; it was so evident that they bring out the best in one another.

Scott met Lisa at a social gathering of mutual friends. What if either of them had declined to go out that fateful evening? Their chance meeting might not have ever happened, but it did. They found out later they had run in the same circle of friends for years but had never met; Lisa had heard his name mentioned before by her friends in passing because one of her friends worked with Scott and one worked for him. On the evening in question, Scott took an immediate liking to Lisa. He later sent her a text (he got her number through their mutual friend) and asked her to lunch. Lisa was flattered, but the timing wasn't quite right. About a week and a half later when the timing was better, Lisa asked him if his offer for lunch was still on the table. Not only did they go out to lunch, but they also went to—get this—an Edward Jones' investment dinner. They had to sit through the presentation, but they managed to find time for conversation too; where there's a will, I guess there's a way. They hit it off. Their first date was on October twenty-fifth, and they were married December sixteenth of the same year!

Scott has three brothers, two sons, and a mom whom he moved this past year to live closer to him. He is very easygoing. He enjoys spending time with family, being on the lake, being on the go, and rising early in the morning to spend time with his bride before she goes to work. He doesn't have to be at his office until, well, until he says so because he's his own boss. She gets up five-thirty every morning, however.

Scott worked for Wal-Mart for twenty-one years. His last role was as a regional manager. Today he is a successful co-owner and principal broker for Berkshire Hathaway. He works hard, but he enjoys what he is doing. If you live in Bentonville, Arkansas, or are planning to move there, Scott is your guy. Visit his website at www.BHHSSolutionsRE.com.

I asked him what he enjoys doing besides working. He looks forward to getting together with twelve to twenty of his frat brothers once a year to float the Buffalo River, which is known as the first national river to be designated in the U.S. He said they used to float a keg of beer behind them in a canoe, but now that they are older, they alternate between beer and water. Sounds like wisdom to me.

Scott's other hobbies include boating, golfing, biking, tending to flowers and landscaping. He and Lisa enjoy going on walks together, going out to listen to various musicians, and inviting friends and family to visit them at their lake house. It is really neat to hear about how their blended family is starting to come together. Scott's twenty-four-year-old and Lisa's twenty-year-old like to go out and do things with them. They feel blessed to have found each other at this stage in their lives, and it is truly a joy to spend time with them. Please, meet Scott and my very dear friend, Lisa.

I had a lovely coffee with Kimberly. We have a few things in common. For starters, I think her family has great taste in names. When she came over to the house, turns out we also have the same taste in floor plans. I met Kimberly towards the end of a party, and we decided to meet for coffee later.

Kimberly is married to Ben and has a six-year-old son. She met Ben in tenth grade, and they became high school sweethearts and eventually married. It hit home as we started to talk. Think about that for a moment: she shared that she knew her brother-in-law since he was five years old and watched him grow up; he is now twenty-five. That also explains why she feels exceptionally close to her mother-in-law; she was probably about fifteen or sixteen when they met. Kimberly and Ben's families are both great support systems for them.

Kimberly did well in school. People used to try to sit by her to copy off of her paper. That is what she thought when Ben started sitting next to her halfway through their sophomore year of high school, but she was wrong. He sat next to her day after day because he liked her. Then, one day in February he got up the courage to ask her for her phone number when they were leaving English class. When she agreed to give it to him, he pulled out the tiniest piece of yellow paper to write it down. He has, since then, forever kept that yellow piece of paper in his wallet. He later told her that was the happiest day that he had ever had to that point. Though they didn't get married until a few years after college, they have been together at the time of this writing for twenty-one years.

Kimberly describes herself as an extrovert; Ben, on the other hand, is an introvert. She said she loves people. When she goes to the store, if he is going to be with her, Ben will tell her to go in, get what she needs, and come out. (That sounds similar to something Joel would have said to me years ago. Perhaps Joel has just given up.)

Kimberly has been in the mortgage industry for eighteen years and has seen it through its ups and downs. What she loves most about it is that there are a lot of happy endings, and she can help make someone's dreams come true. When they have to turn someone down for a loan, they are looking out for them in the long run (the bank too).

Kimberly and Ben used to live in a subdivision known as Olympic Heights. Every street in that area was named after an Olympic athlete. They moved when they realized they needed a home better suited to their growing family. Kimberly is an only child and said she was used to getting her way. Their son is an only child too, so she jokingly said Ben has an uphill battle. Kimberly enjoys volunteering at her son's school and decorating her home for the holidays. She shared that Ben spoils her and lets her go all out for Halloween and Christmas.

Kimberly and the women in her family, about ten of them, have supported the Susan B. Komen Race for the Cure for the past fifteen years. They go all out and start planning in the summer for the race. Each year, they come up with a theme and T-shirts. This past year was her favorite theme: butterflies. Afterward, they treat themselves to brunch at the Cheesecake Factory; it has become a family tradition. Please, meet Kimberly.

I met Corey and Jie at the library by simply asking them if they would take a picture of Sarah and me. You met Sarah in Chapter 6. Jie took the picture, and then they were herding their three little girls out of the library; I was right behind them leaving also. Their little girls are adorable, so being a mom, of course, I had to comment. Corey is a friendly person, so we struck up a conversation about children. Jie and Corey have a charming story.

Jie is from China. You pronounce her name "gee ah" with sound lifting on the second syllable. She and Corey met online. Yes, you read that right: online while Corey was living in the U.S. After corresponding for a year, Corey took a trip to China to meet her. He said that when they met, it did not feel like work talking to her; they hit it off right away. Corey came back to the U.S. for a bit, but shortly after that he quit his regular job and moved to China. They dated for five years before they got married. He had been running a business part-time but took it on full-bore once he moved. I'll tell you about his business in a little bit because that story is interesting also.

Corey and Jie moved to the United States ten years ago, and they settled in New Hampshire. Jie said it was freezing and a hard move for her. She lost ten pounds in the process because she could not get used to American food, and she couldn't understand what people were saying. It helped that Corey had lived in China for some time. He was able to understand what Jie missed about home, and that made things better. Jie said they had each other, and that helped a lot. Very sweet.

The two of them moved to Austin in 2010. It is a much better environment for her, and she loves it here! Corey and Jie have three daughters. The oldest is six, and they have twin girls who are four. They used to travel back and forth to China quite a bit until the kids started school. The girls can speak both Chinese and English well, but because they want to blend in, they only speak English while in America, and they only speak Chinese when they are in China: they are normal kids wanting to fit in. Corey is fluent in Chinese, and Jie is fluent in English. They must interpret for their parents when the in-laws are together because neither of their parents speaks the other's language.

Corey and Jie own a business selling portable washing machines. They sell ten- and twenty-pound small laundry appliances for RV's, boats, apartments and the like. The business idea was born when Corey moved to a flat (before he met Jie). He had to share a washer and had to split the bill with a neighbor who had eight children. They were washing all of the time. Just to use the machine was going to cost him $175 a month. Instead, he searched and finally found a portable one in South Africa. He convinced the supplier to sell him one machine, then fifty. Thus, his business began.

Corey said he never thought he could start his own company, but it just sort-of happened. Now he sells them in China too; you know what they say about necessity being the mother of invention. Jie helps him in the business. He says he gives her all of the complicated, tricky deals. She does the hard negotiations in China. She also does the bookkeeping and helps with the strategy. They have made it work as a team. If you need a portable washer or dryer, you're in luck! You can buy one at www. laundry-alternative.com.

Jie has adapted to life in America; she has even become a foodie! She loves Thai and Italian and is open to experimenting with new tastes. Corey enjoys basketball, but it seems his favorite hobby is gathering pecans from parks and making homemade pies from them. Please, meet Corey, Jie, and two of their girls. (Their oldest daughter was shy, so she didn't want to take her picture.)

I was on my way to the gym when I passed by Mandy and two others at her turquoise table. I rolled down my window to say hello to Mandy when she introduced me to her parents, who were visiting. They were here to celebrate their granddaughter Ellie's fifth birthday. You met Mandy, Craig, and Ellie in Chapter 7. Her parents were friendly, so I asked Mandy if she thought her parents would be willing to share their story. She volunteered them, so I parked the car and joined them at her turquoise table.

RAY'S STORY:

Ray comes from a large family, being one of seven children. His father will be one hundred this coming year: March 2019. His father is one of the last WWII veterans living and lives in his own home. He grew up during the depression in a time when you did everything for yourself. I asked Ray what he thought his father's secret to a long and healthy life was. He laughed then told me his father doesn't keep anything inside. If his father is mad at you, you know it; he doesn't sugar coat anything, so he carries no pent-up frustrations. He was married for more than fifty years, so I guess this worked well for him.

Ray is from Sealy, Texas. His first job was working at a car dealership where he was successful. The individual who hired him became very instrumental in Ray's life. You'll understand just how important in a minute. For now, we'll call him Mr. U.

Mr. U. was so impressed with Ray that every time he moved to a new dealership, he would bring Ray along. It was at the dealership in Sealy that Ray met his future wife, Barb. She came in and caught his eye. It turns out Mr. U. is Barb's uncle! Ray was so smitten, he asked Mr. U if he could ask Barb out on a date. Her uncle gave his approval, so Ray asked Barb to be his date for his brother's wedding. His version of the story is that she didn't know what she was in for because she was a Baptist girl getting ready to go to a Catholic wedding.

Ray was excited to tell me about his first date with Barb. When he first asked her out, she hesitated. She called her uncle first to get his advice. Her uncle approved but with a caveat: he told her that Ray liked to dance—a lot. That didn't bother her, but she was independent, so she insisted on driving her vehicle. She did not want him to pick her up from her home—a first for Ray for sure. She drove her car to her uncle's house, so Ray had to pick her up and return her to his boss' home. No pressure!

Ray currently teaches at a school that certifies pipeline weld inspectors. He has been happily married for twenty-eight years and is now the proud grandfather of three. His life is full of his farm and his grandchildren. Ellie, Mandy's daughter, is the youngest, and in his words, "rules the roost!" When I asked him about hobbies, he said he shreds, burns, and mows. That's when I learned his farm is twenty acres.

BARB'S STORY:

Barb is from Jamestown, Tennessee. She moved to Texas more than thirty years ago and worked for an orthodontist the majority of that time. She was a single parent of two daughters when she met Ray. Barb has one brother and two sisters, and her mom still lives in her own home and has been there for sixty years.

Barb reminisced about growing up in the country, swinging on grapevines and working in the garden every summer. She enjoyed her childhood so much, she said she would live her childhood all over again without changing a thing. That would be music to any parent's ears. Ray commented that her mom and dad were the "salt of the earth." Barb's dad passed away seven years ago.

When Ray asked Barb out, she joked that she turned him down two or three times; Ray just chuckled and exclaimed he wasn't used to being turned down. As her girls were growing up, she loved being involved with their school activities and going on soccer trips. Their schedule was hectic, but she misses those days. When Mandy, the youngest daughter, left home, it was hard for Barb and Ray to adjust. They had to work at reconnecting because they had made Molly and Mandy their central focus.

Now that both girls are settled and raising their own children, Barb and Ray have transitioned into a different stage. As they prepare for retirement, they are trying to figure their next steps. Barb believes she will probably do volunteer work: perhaps at a school. Ray will likely continue to teach in some capacity. Please, meet the funny and delightful Ray and Barbara.

Joel and our son, Dillon, were at a sports bar watching a game and having a bite to eat when they met a friendly couple sitting nearby. They started talking about the game and had a great chat. Joel came home, told me about this couple, then handed me their number and told me to give them a call. They were up for my challenge. Way to go, Joel! He stepped right out of his comfort zone. It helped that Josh and Valerie were open to conversation. Joel told me Josh's outgoing personality was very similar to mine.

Josh grew up in Allen, Texas, which is a northern suburb of Dallas and has an older brother. He went to the University of Texas where he earned a degree in Mechanical Engineering. Josh worked for a year in Austin, got married, then relocated to Massachusetts for work. He liked it enough; that is until winter showed up. Coming from Texas, he was not used to going to work in the dark and returning home in the dark. Josh said he never saw the sun. After the year there, he returned to Austin.

Valerie is also from Dallas, has an older brother, and went to the University of Texas to get her degree in graphic design. But that was right when computers exploded on the scene. She had no idea graphic design jobs would now require her to sit behind a computer for eight hours a day. That was not her cup of tea. She loved it when it was cut and paste and taking pictures. After graduating, Valerie worked a couple of jobs, got married, then moved to Massachusetts. A year later, she returned to Austin too.

If it seems like Josh and Valerie have a lot in common, they do. They both attended Skyline High School and started dating September thirteenth of their senior year. Josh remembers that date! It was a pre-date for homecoming. Josh told me he had never gone to any school dances before and that one of his best friends, Chris Turner, a current state representative, was encouraging him to ask someone to go with him to homecoming. Right then, Valerie parked near them. So, Josh quickly decided to ask her to homecoming. (He had been kind of sweet on Valerie since their freshmen year but never acted on that attraction.) To ensure Valerie would say yes before he asked her to the dance, he solicited the help of another friend, Roderick. Roderick's assignment was simple: ask Valerie the hypothetical question, "If Josh asked you to homecoming, would you say yes?" Roderick accepted his mission and left. When Josh and Roderick talked later, Roderick assured Josh that he would be happy with the result when he asked Valerie to homecoming. This answer led Josh to believe Roderick had spoken to Valerie. He had not! If this seems like high school sort of stuff: remember, it was.

When Josh finally asked Valerie to the homecoming dance, her response was, "I need to think about that." Unbeknownst to Josh, she already had a date for homecoming, (Incidentally, he was an older boy also named Josh). Valerie thought to herself, *It would probably be better to go with a high school guy.* Within minutes, she accepted younger Josh's invitation with, "OK, yeah." Valerie's response led to their first date, a "homecoming pre-date," which later turned into seven years of dating with a couple of breaks, to now twenty-one years of marriage, and two children: a daughter, who is currently a freshman in college, and a son, who is a sophomore in high school.

After moving back to Austin, Josh worked in semiconducting, high-tech engineering for a computer chip manufacturer. He did that until he took over his father's business, Rope Works, Inc., fifteen years ago. They do inspections for commercial zip lines all over the U.S. and along the cruise ship stops such as Costa Rica, Jamaica, and Belize. They also build challenge courses for summer camps where you can have an adventure up in the air. My impression of zip lines was that they were used for an adrenalin rush of fun; while they are used for recreation, Josh and Valerie opened my eyes to the other practical applications which can increase the quality of life for many different groups of people in society.

After 9/11, a lot of parents were sending their children to camps where ziplining and similar confidence-building activities were used to help kids begin to trust again. Juvenile detention centers use them in this way too. Josh and Valerie are currently working on a project for Wounded Warriors to help soldiers who come back injured regain a sense of community and acclimate in a measured way. Being able to participate in these types of exciting activities with other individuals who've had similar or shared experiences provides a structured environment for veterans to talk with others who understand the challenges of transitioning into their "new normal."

In addition to that, The Extravaganza, an annual event held in Dallas, is one of the events Josh and Valerie put on that includes zip lines and challenging activities for people with disabilities. Setting up for this event allows Josh to use his engineering background to make adaptations in new and existing equipment to accommodate various needs.

Josh and Valerie also shared that they know most of the other zip line builders because it's a small industry. They often work together, sharing knowledge and information and sometimes workers when it makes sense. They believe when one wins, they all win: that collaborative competition makes their industry better. If you are interested in zipping, check out their websites, www.ropeworksinc.com and www.ziplostpines.com. Please, meet Josh and Valerie.

I met Chris at the same friend's get together, where I met Kirk (Chapter 5). Chris was born in San Antonio and moved to Austin when he was seven. He has an identical twin brother and a sister who is seven years older than them. Chris is married and has two daughters. He attended Texas A&M where he earned both his undergraduate degree in finance and a master's in international affairs, specializing in international economics and development.

After college, Chris went to work for Grant Thornton in Houston where he worked in their international transfer pricing department. Though he learned a lot, Houston was not his cup of tea; he prayed about why he was there. Through a networking contact, just before layoffs were about to hit his department, Chris was transferred to the business valuation department. Here he got the opportunity to rub elbows with a lot of CEO's and VP's and help them evaluate the worth of their company to sell it. This department was clear across the other side of the building from his first job, which was significant because people on one side did not run into the people from the other side.

The first day of his new position, Chris met his future wife, Katie. Evidently, he sat down at the wrong desk—the desk of a friend of hers—and she wasn't too pleased about it. (Katie told him later she was quite annoyed with him.) She didn't let on she was miffed but politely told him he needed to move. In whatever way Chris responded to her, it worked. She invited him to join the volleyball team she had started, and later she invited him to go to salsa and country-western dancing. One thing led to another, and they began dating. (Okay, so now I'd like to hear her side of it.) That was ten years ago, and Chris says, "It's been awesome!"

Shortly after he married, Chris' father asked for his help in a big transition for his company, Retirement Counselors, Inc. After helping his Dad, Chris discovered that he thoroughly enjoyed this work and helping others in this way. He is now a financial advisor with his father and said, "It's pretty cool." Chris also told me he is an advisor endorsed by Dave Ramsey. If you would like Chris' help, you can find him at, www.retirementcounselors.net.

I asked Chris what it was like to be an identical twin. "It is one of the coolest things in the world! It is awesome! If God could make you your best friend from birth: same thing. They agree with you on everything—they hate the same people you do, and they love the same food. I mean, if you want someone to just think you're awesome, have a twin because they think they're awesome, and so it is so much fun." Of course, growing up, they did the typical switch-a-roo with their classes, and now even their children will get them mixed up. They are not allowed to play the game Catch Phrase together anymore because they were so good at guessing what the other one was trying to say that it wasn't fair to the rest of the players. Ironically, when they get together, they talk non-stop. They have so much to say to each other; that part boggled my mind. I asked him if it was like having a conversation with himself. "Yes. It really, really is! I can call him up because I want his opinion about something, but I already know how I feel, and he'll tell me how I feel because that's how he feels."

Every year for their birthday, they ask their wives for one weekend together to hang out, talk about life, and catch up. Chris also said though, that for each of them, they both consider their typical best weekends are when they get to be home with their wives and kids. Outside of work, Chris enjoys house projects and landscaping; he likes using his hands to build something. His absolute favorite, though, is being in the yard digging in the dirt, planting trees and bushes, and cutting down and burning cedar.

Just as we were winding down our conversation, I asked him if he had any unique experiences he thought would be interesting for you to know about, and he told me about several of his graduate school experiences. First, he was able to study Japanese as part of a language immersion program in Middlebury, Vermont, for three weeks. You couldn't write, read, see, or hear English in any form, or you would be expelled from the program. He knew he was picking up the language when he started to dream in Japanese! Second, he had the opportunity to study in both China and India and had the chance to sit down with some of their government leaders and heads of state. While in New Delhi, India, he was able to see the sunrise come over the Himalayan Mountains and experienced an "attack" of wild monkeys. (There were a lot of wild monkeys on the mountain that would start to charge them periodically, but the dogs the tour guides had would chase them away.) Finally, one of his good friends that started Motorola in Japan set up a private meeting for him with Bob Gates a few months before Gates became the Secretary of Defense.

He was not sure how some of these opportunities came about but is very thankful they did. Please, meet Chris.

My husband, Joel, introduced me to Paul and Sharon. He kept telling me, "You've gotta meet this couple and get their story." He was right. They both have an incredible sense of humor and are very down to earth.

Sharon was born in London, and Paul is from the Bronx. They met on a blind date in England. Sharon's co-worker, Vanessa, set her up with her boyfriend's roommate, Paul. All Sharon knew was that her date was an American GI who had black hair and brown eyes, and his nickname was Pemo. Meanwhile, Paul had been asking his roommate, Chuck, about Sharon. Chuck was no help because he had never met Sharon before.

Sharon tells the story that Paul and Chuck drove up in a "mini." She noticed they made three passes around the traffic circle. It turns out Paul was trying to see what Sharon looked like. He had told Chuck that if Sharon wasn't pretty, he wouldn't stop but rather keep going. Paul said each time he passed by her, the only thing he could see was her long hair and legs. He decided since her legs looked okay, he'd take a gamble and stop. During their double date, Vanessa and Chuck began arguing and broke up that very night. Ironically, Chuck was later the best man at Paul and Sharon's wedding.

At the end of the evening, Paul asked Sharon if he could see her again. He asked if he could take her out the next night. She said, "Sorry, I'm going to a party with my friends. I'm busy." He said, "How about the next night, the day after, a week later, one month from today, six months from today?"

To each request, Sharon answered with, "I'm busy," or some variation thereof.

Chuck, the roommate, told Sharon later that after Paul got back in the car, he said to him, "I'm going to marry her." The next day, Paul showed up at Sharon's mother's house.

Her mother answered the door and told her, "There's some American here for you." Sharon had been planning to go to the dance with her friends that night. She thought, *Okay, he can pay for me to get into the dance. I'll get a few drinks, he can buy my girlfriends drinks, and then I'll dump him.* We'll have to forgive Sharon these thoughts. She was only sixteen at the time, and the GI's in her English town had a bad reputation for how they treated the girls.

Sharon went to the dance with Paul, but all night long she avoided him. Her girlfriends were in on it and helped her efforts. When Paul would ask them which way she went as he was buying them a drink, they would then send him to the opposite side of the dance hall from where she was. He said he spent the whole night being a human ping pong ball. Finally, it dawned on him that he was being played, so when Sharon's girlfriends told him they saw her in one direction, he went in the other. He said he found her, and it was "Game over!"

When people hear their story of how they met, Sharon is often asked when she decided she liked him. Her standard reply is, "I'm still trying to figure that out." Both she and Paul were laughing as she said this. Paul chimed in, "I grew on her like a wart." Too funny; they have been happily married for forty-six years. It was less than a month after the dance that Paul asked Sharon to marry him: she was seventeen. When they got married, they had only known each other for six months.

Paul got out of the Air Force, and they moved to New York three months after their wedding. Folks, are you getting that at seventeen Sharon not only got married, but she also moved a continent away from her family and everything she knew? (At seventeen, I got homesick when I moved from Baltimore to Colorado Springs.) They lived in New York for five years then moved back to England for thirteen years. While in England, they had their two daughters and were co-owners, with her parents, of a pizzeria and bed and breakfast. The pizzeria started as a bakery; Sharon's parents were professional chefs. It evolved into a pizzeria when one day Sharon announced she was going to make a pizza. That was her New York experience coming out. She accidentally made too much pizza, so she put some in their store window. It sold like crazy. Very naturally they transitioned into a pizzeria. The pizza was such a novelty that it sold cold right out of the window! Paul said people couldn't even pronounce it. They were calling it pizzah.

A LITTLE ABOUT SHARON SPECIFICALLY:

Sharon's father had been in the British Air Force, so they (mom, dad, and brother) had moved around a lot. They once lived in Africa—Kenya, in fact—for three-and-a-half years near the end of the Mau Mau uprising. It was a dangerous time. Her family lived near two different villages. One was friendly, but the other was not. The village that was not was very pro-independence and had killed a little English child that had gone into their village. For this reason, her family knew not to go there. The other village was safe, and Sharon remembers playing with the children and speaking Swahili.

One Christmas Eve Sharon was baking sausage rolls with her mother. When she looked out the window, she saw the people of the unfriendly village surrounding her house. A spear was thrown through their window, and the villagers set fire to their home with them inside! It was people from the friendly village that came and chased the others off, put the fire out, and rescued them. Close call for sure!

Sharon recently retired from the U.S. postal service after working there for twenty years. She enjoys doing embroidery, and her finished works are quite beautiful.

A LITTLE ABOUT PAUL:

Paul's mother practiced tough love and kicked him out of the house when he was not doing right as a teenager. She said the only way he could get back in the house was to join the Air Force like his cousins had done. After living on the street for two days, he agreed and signed up for the Air Force.

Paul is a "creative" and situationally aware person. He was so "creative" that he got into the Air Force under age, without his diploma or GED, and partially blind in one eye. He says that during the Vietnam era, many rules were, shall we say, "somewhat relaxed." Hmmm—along the lines of being "creative," Paul was able to get a military driver's license in England without even having a state one issued in the U.S. (remember he was from New York where having a car to get around is not a necessity). He lost that license, eventually. There is a funny story about how Paul got another license later in New York and one in England—all above board—but sadly, I don't have room to tell it here.

Paul said that during his time in the Air Force, he was surrounded by a lot of super educated people and not the kind of people he had hung out with while living in the Bronx. They kept giving him books to read he had never heard of before. He also told me stories about his time in Vietnam. Some were funny, and some very serious. He did say he feels very fortunate.

Paul is a guitarist, singer, and songwriter. He played a sample of some of his songs for me and even gave me one of his CD's. There is one song, in particular, that is very special. I am convinced it would go viral because it speaks to a shared emotional experience. It is called The Empty Room and is about his daughter leaving home for good to be on her own. If the right producer would hear that song—wow! Please, meet Paul and Sharon.

11

NETWORKING TIPS: PRACTICAL STEPS

"Networking is Goodworking"

—Don Orlando

Meeting people becomes a stress-free behavior to adopt as a daily routine if you flip the focus from *what you can get* to *what you can give*. Try it. I think one reason the idea of "networking" is awkward or uncomfortable for some is that their motive and approach is, *what's in it for me* versus *what I can do to help you*. When was the last time you encountered someone uninterested in talking about themselves or met an individual who rejected assistance that could benefit them? Once you change the reflective lens, it truly becomes easy.

Tips for meeting people:

Smile!

> A smile can go a very long way. Several people I encountered in this challenge were sitting at communal tables in coffee

shops. There were other people I could have asked to be in my challenge, but the reason I asked the person I did was that they seemed more friendly and approachable in some way. Usually, it was their genuine smile or their willingness to make eye contact.

Body language matters.

If someone was hunched over or displaying closed body language, I was less likely to approach them. Be aware of the signals you are sending to others subconsciously. According to body language expert, Mark Bowden, from the moment someone sees you—within seconds—they start to put you into one of four categories: friend, foe, indifferent, or potential mate.

Warm introductions are preferred.

I was more likely to make a lasting connection at an event or through a mutual friend versus just random connections at a gym or store.

Be interesting. Ask open-ended questions.

Being interested in others made me interesting. At parties, people were intrigued about my quest to meet others, what techniques I used that were successful, and the stories I was hearing.

Spending time with others = value to others.

It is harder to form a meaningful connection with a short meeting. If I wanted to get to know someone, it was better to set up a separate meeting where there was adequate time to visit and let the conversation grow organically.

One-on-one conversations are the best for connecting.

With that in mind, at a party or networking event, I could have a more meaningful conversation with two or three people individually than trying to have a meaningful conversation with everyone. It is much more productive to have fewer conversations that lead to follow-up conversations than it is to meet everyone and grab twenty business cards.

People you know, know other people.

Often people in my orbit of associations were able to open doors for me to meet other people I would need or want to know. They introduced me to more than just a few. If you are married, your spouse can also be a great source of wonderful connections. This leads me to my next point.

Make connections for other people.

Remember the variation of Newton's 3rd law. Sometimes I have been able to connect two people I met where there is a mutual benefit, or one person might be an excellent resource for another.

The more people you make an effort to meet, the more comfortable you will become introducing yourself to others. Always look for opportunities to expand your network while being mindful that who you associate with matters.

Don't take the latter statement the wrong way. I do not mean size people up by your perception of their station in life. I mean, look at the quality of their character. People you associate with can lead you to other opportunities or may cause doors to close. Your network is a reflection on you.

Your social media matters tremendously—even what you say in groups or on pages.

Your posts are what others will use to construct what they think your brand is. When individuals wanted to follow my challenge, they would often send me a friend request on Facebook. Before I would accept their request, I would check out their page to see what types of things they were posting.

Join organizations and get involved; this includes volunteering.

Friends and associates within organizations I belong to willingly and regularly introduced me to new people. Your world will open up.

Do fun things and include others.

Be intentional about the people who come across your path as you do life.

Tips for deepening relationships:

Follow Up.

Something to keep in mind: developing good relationships beyond just meeting someone will take time. This is where many people drop the ball. To deepen the relationship beyond the initial meeting, depending on how and where I met someone, I follow up with them. There are many ways you can follow up, some more personal than others. I will often follow up with people through social media by engaging with their posts or sending them a private message. In some cases, I will send an email, text, or make an effort to reconnect in person. I take my cues from the person and how open they are to build a relationship.

Give without any expectation of anything in return.

If you give this way, you avoid unmet expectations. Often when people experience disappointment or even hurt in a relationship, it is because they had unspoken and/or unmet expectations. Besides, when you give in a calculating way, the other person can eventually, if not immediately, get this vibe from you.

Ask for small favors.

This does not conflict with giving without any expectation. When you ask for a favor, are upfront about it, and you truly give the other person the freedom to say no, the other person feels needed and valued. They are more inclined to do another favor for you. This is known as the Benjamin Franklin effect. However, keep in mind the bank account analogy. If you make too many withdrawals, the opposite will occur, and you will become known as the taker that we talked about in Chapter 7.

Look for commonalities.

It can be a common interest, a hobby, a value, etc. It can literally be anything you can bond over.

12

NETWORKING DEFINED

"You can make more friends in two months by becoming interested in other people than you can in two years by trying to get other people interested in you."

—Dale Carnegie

I am passionate about meeting new people. When I meet new people, I get the opportunity to learn and grow. I am able to experience life through someone else's eyes. I learn about things I've never done and places I've never been. The 100-day challenge was the most amazing experience I've ever had—well next to getting married, childbirth, and jumping out of a plane. Truly, it was pretty awesome! The conversations were rich and powerful, and I am forever changed.

As a result of this challenge, many people would say I am good at networking. But what does that really mean? What is your definition of networking? Some say it is meeting specific people that can help you. Others say it's simply expanding your sphere of influence. I say networking is relationship building. Building relationships involves three elements:

1. Building Social Capital
2. Being Mindful & Intentional
3. Paying attention to Every Single Human Interaction

Networking = Relationship Building (Rel. Bldg.)

Rel. Bldg. =	Building Social Capital	+	Being Mindful	+	Every Human Interaction

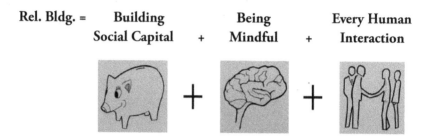

I define social capital as those intangible assets that offer value such as appreciation, expertise, helpfulness, knowledge, influence, insight, and time.

Building Social Capital = Offering Intangible Assets of Value
(Appreciation, Expertise, Helpfulness, Knowledge, Influence, Insight, Time)

The same concept I explained about my view on having a happy marriage in Chapter 10 applies to networking—the bank account analogy where you make many more deposits than withdrawals. In other words, focus on giving versus taking from someone you encounter. It will come back to you. It may not come back from where you sowed it directly, but it will come back. During my challenge, I built social capital by offering my time and showing appreciation for someone's story.

Now let's look at the second element—being mindful. This concept is simple: pay attention to those that come across your path and listen to connect with those same people. It is having the intentional mindset to give attention to people wherever you go. Whether it is the coffee shop (one of my favorite places—I'd sit at a communal table); the library; a car show; a birthday party (whether it is for an adult and child); a car dealership (while getting your car worked on); a grocery store; Home Depot; office supply store; your child's sporting event or practice; yoga class; cycling group; golfing, a book club; or professional associations, pay attention. My point is that we encounter lots of people in many of the places we frequent during the day. There are plenty of opportunities to meet new people if we are intentional about doing so.

The third and final element is being aware of every single human interaction. In short, when building relationships, we must be present or "in the moment" in every conversation or encounter we have with another person. How do you make someone feel? What's coming across to them: Are you sincere? Do you have an ulterior motive? Do they sense confidence in you or timidity? Is what you say congruent with your actions? Have you ever caught yourself disingenuously saying, "We'll need to invite you over for dinner," but then you never do? Do you tell someone you will do something and then don't? I am certainly not perfect, but I strive to live by the motto: If I don't mean it, don't say it." What about the voicemails you leave? Posts you make? Or emails you send?

To help illustrate my point, I will share a brief email exchange I had recently. This example highlights the importance of being mindful with every interaction. Admittedly, I was in a hurry and wasn't being present or attentive of my interaction with a colleague.

Initial email:

> *"Hi, Kymberli,*
> *My business partner and I founded an Emotional Intelligence training company, and we are starting to grow our team. We are looking for coaches. If you are interested, let's set up a zoom for next week. I look forward to hearing from you. Have a great day!"*

My response:

> *"Hi, Samantha,*
> *I would be interested in hearing more about what you do. My next available time would be in the afternoon on Thursday, May 30th. It is an office afternoon, so I will have flexibility. Let me know what time would work for you.*
> *Kind regards,*
> *Kymberli"*

I never received a reply to my response. So, I reread my email and decided I should send a follow-up.

My revised response:

> *"I was in a bit of a hurry packing for a trip when I sent my response. Just reread it and wanted to circle back with you. My apologies for the shortness of it! I am out of town this week and am working on a few deadlines when I get back. I would love to "meet" you on Zoom. Angela said you and Melanie are good people. :-) What I had meant to say in my email was May 30th on, I have much greater flexibility to meet. Would a time in the afternoon on the 30th or a date later work for you?*
> *Looking forward to hearing about your company, your vision, and how I may be of help!*
> *Kind regards,*
> *Kymberli"*

Not surprising. There was an immediate response!

Their reply:

> *"Hi, Kymberli,*
> *Your response was just right. Let's circle back around in early June. Have a great trip!"*

In the first response, I was distracted. My second response, I was intentionally mindful and present. So that gets back to my definition of networking.

Networking = Relationship Building (Rel. Bldg.)

Rel. Bldg. = Building Social Capital + Being Mindful+ Every Human Interaction

13

LESSONS TO MYSELF—THINGS I DISCOVERED OR SIMPLY OBSERVED

"Life gives us experiences for personal development. Appreciate the lessons and be a learner."

—Lailah Gifty Akita

Newton's 3rd Law: For every action, there is an equal and opposite reaction.

➤ I discovered a variation of Newton's 3rd law of motion— Generally speaking, I found that for every "kind" action, there is an equal and reciprocating reaction. It was easy to set in motion the kindness in people by first being friendly and authentic.

❖ I began my approach and interaction with a genuine smile. Many were willing to help me, a total stranger accomplish a goal.

❖ People respond well to others who genuinely take an interest in them. Friends and colleagues were amazed at the breadth and depth people shared about their lives in such a short encounter with someone they just met.

❖ My husband offered to help a friend clear some of his land. They, in turn, invited both of us over for dinner. While there, they introduced me to a neighbor whom I got to include in this project. Sowing seeds without the expectation of something in return produces fruit; the fruit may not always be produced where you initially sowed it, but it will eventually come up somewhere.

Being Extrospective:

➢ The more "extrospective" I became each day, the more I learned about programs and opportunities in the local community. People I meet often tell me about business opportunities or groups they belong to without my asking about them. People feel appreciated that I want to hear their story, and they want to give me something back.

➢ When we only pay attention to our own story, if something unfortunate happens, we might be tempted to think we're the only ones that got the short end of the stick.

➢ I have been unaware of the magnitude of pain a significant number of people carry daily.

➢ I ran into all kinds of people from many different backgrounds. By seeking to understand their perspective, people often then asked me mine and showed a genuine interest in what I had to say.

➢ I began to see people in my community that I had met previously in my challenge. I would see them at the local

Goin' Postal store, at the coffee shop, at the grocery store, or a restaurant, and we would be glad to see each other; it was like we were old friends. That is likely because by being intentional in our conversation, it was as if we had spent a few years together versus a few minutes or hours.

➤ Many individuals expressed a deep appreciation of someone caring enough to ask them about their story. When they would say, "Thank you for asking me about my story," I felt their appreciation profoundly. I realized they had shared something precious to them, and that it was I who had received a great gift and honor.

Being Human—the common experience:

➤ Everyone I met was in the same human condition: imperfect human beings living in an imperfect world, faced with life's everyday challenges.

➤ What connects us is our stories. When someone is sensitive to our story, we form a bond with them.

➤ Others will open up and share when they realize you don't have an ulterior motive: you are genuinely interested in them as a person and not trying to get something out of them or from them.

➤ Based on the feedback from people I spoke with, writing their story and highlighting the positives encouraged them to see themselves differently. That is the same response I often got when I would write someone's resume; it helped them see themselves from a different perspective.

➤ No one's life is without some rain, regardless of how positive their story is told. Sometimes you have to read between the lines. I only point this out because people tend to judge their own story against someone else's. Don't. You will only see what someone else shows you. No one can have it all.

➢ The people who had severe circumstances have told me that what helped them the most was avoiding isolation and realizing they were not alone in their situation.

➢ Life can be hard and filled with huge disappointments, but the human spirit wants to rise.

➢ Regardless of race, gender, economic circumstances, we all have hurt. We can all benefit from sharing our story with someone trustworthy.

➢ In a time when the narrative is negative, and the country is seemingly divided (2018), I am meeting people from all types of backgrounds, and I am finding we have more in common than we have different.

➢ We are all just people trying our best to make it through life the best way we can. We all have different starting points. Trying to understand where someone is coming from will help in understanding the choices they make.

➢ We all need encouragement. No one operates in a vacuum. It was great to wake up each day to people cheering me on. When I doubted my ability to complete the 100-day challenge, I would receive needed encouragement. Side note: Social media can quickly become addictive!

Personal Growth & Observations:

➢ I changed personally. After twenty-two days, my husband said he had noticed a subtle change in me since I started this project. I asked him what it was, and he said I had developed a quiet sense of confidence, purpose, and the ability to establish rapport with people in seconds.

➢ I don't recommend making decisions about someone based on first impressions. Initial impressions of someone cannot tell their story: hence, who they are. During my challenge, not once could I predict what someone's story was going to entail.

➢ The more I spent time meeting people and attentively listening to their stories, the better conversationalist I became. Said another way, one key to people finding you interesting has a lot to do with you being interested in them: to live in the curious. When I go to a party now, people are more interested in what I have to say. The more I sit and listen, the more others gravitate towards me.

➢ I met some people with different value systems than mine, and some were far different. The world is full of different people. In the last section, Being Human, I mentioned we all have different starting points, but where the personal growth comes in is when I came up against the far different value systems. It made me stop to think about my values and where those values came from—that it may be wise to examine my experiences to identify how my values developed and if they are still valid. It also made me think about how I react to others who don't hold my same values.

➢ The question that came up at least three times when talking to those in their later twenties was, "Why not?" I find myself wondering, "Why not?" What are my limiting beliefs, and are those well-founded?

➢ If someone has lost a loved one, I learned that in many cases the subject of a lost loved one was not off-limits; they want to be able to talk about that person—to be able to hear their names and share insights and stories with others about them. Every person I spoke to during this challenge who has suffered the loss of a loved one has thanked me for listening to their story.

➢ When you are vulnerable with others (not to be confused with oversharing), this will deepen a relationship. Often vulnerability will be reciprocated.

➢ Poor is relative. That is to say, it struck me that there are varying degrees of being poor. I have come across many people in my life who describe their upbringing that way. I have been fortunate to have never experienced poverty. I found myself going to the dictionary to understand this term better. Here is one definition I found. "Lacking sufficient money to live at a standard considered comfortable or normal in a society." What one considers comfortable or normal is not standard across the board.

➢ I heard three stories of the loss of a loved one in twenty-six hours: one person I knew before this challenge, the other two I met during the challenge. At the risk of sounding cliché, I should tell the ones I love that I love them as often as I can. Tomorrow is not guaranteed. Leave nothing unsaid.

➢ I am a rules follower which has its advantages but taken to the extreme can limit who a person can become. I met people who don't live in fear of rules. They don't take themselves too seriously, which makes room for more laughter and more joy.

➢ It was not uncommon that someone I met already knew someone I was connected to. I always found that to be pretty interesting and it just proves to me that we are only six degrees (or less) from the help we may need at times.

➢ If I could find the person I wrote the story about on Facebook, I would also tag them. Then I noticed their connections' reactions to the stories I posted. My connections would comment, but I would pay particular attention to the comments posted by their friends and family. That told me a lot more about them and their brand: strong, amazing, great mother, fantastic co-worker. It's the nouns and adjectives people choose to use when describing someone that gives a lot of insight into that person's character.

➤ We all have choices about how we tell our story. What you focus on and how you focus on it will determine how your story is told, both by you *and* those around you.

➤ We all want validation from others. I know I am not immune. While social media can be a great way to stay in touch with people, there is a clear and present danger in that it provides immediate and visible feedback of validation or the lack thereof. Our youth, who all want to—and are trying to— fit in, are especially vulnerable to this feedback; and it can be isolating. They now have an immediate metric of how popular they are. When I was growing up, I had a sense of how I fit in, but not a transparent and public indicator.

➤ To gain someone's trust is something to be cherished. Most people were very trusting with their story; only a few wanted to see what I would write before I shared it with the world. Both were right, and in either case, I did my best to steward their stories well.

A FEW FINAL THOUGHTS:

Towards the end of my challenge, several friends asked how I was making connections with others—how was I starting conversations? At the risk of being redundant, the answer is that I am starting from the point of being interested in the other person. That is my only motive. Next, I looked for something, anything, in common, and I asked why and open-ended questions. One of my favorite questions is, "Tell me something you know good." That was a question my father used to ask, and he used those exact words. Of course, there are other ways to ask this same question. Why do I particularly like this question? Because it makes the other person feel good. Even if someone is having a bad day, they will search their minds to tell you something good, which will release the feel-good hormones of oxytocin and serotonin. You will cause them to feel better, and they will then associate you with something that evoked a positive feeling.

Another question I frequently received was—how are you able to connect with people at a deeper level than just exchanging pleasantries in an initial conversation? My simple answer is that whenever I met with someone, I was genuinely interested in that person. People can feel when you disconnect from them, or your attention is divided. Stay present in your conversations. Listen to connect.

Are you an introvert? If you are, you actually have a better chance of being a great networker because introverts generally tend to listen more effectively. I am an extrovert. I love to engage with others, but I want to talk and have to make myself focus on listening. The good news for extroverts is that listening can be a learned skill!

Speaker Kelly Hoey once said that networking is every single human interaction. I would have to agree that that is undoubtedly a significant part of networking. Her statement would address the building of social capital and how you make someone feel aspects of what I consider essential elements of networking. You are continually leaving an impression when you interact with someone—whether it is in person, virtually, by written correspondence; by what you do or fail to do; by how you make someone feel or not feel.

Throughout life, we all need help from time to time. I have found that you never know from where your help will come. Sometimes it is from a friend. Many times it is from a friend of a friend—who then may become a friend, which has certainly been true in my life. But more often than not, it starts with a friend versus a total stranger. And because real friendships take time to develop, my recommendation is to plant your crops before you're hungry. There's no time like the present to expand your network and improve your life.

My experiences as a career coach and personal branding expert have led me to this conclusion: people who are well-connected and well-networked are generally happier people who accomplish more and find employment at a much faster rate than people who aren't. At the very core of networking is the genuine passion for wanting to know others, help others, and build relationships with others. Hence, whenever I come across someone new, my ever-present thought is I need to know you.

Call to action: Now that you've read this book, take action. Be curious. Who are the fifteen to twenty people you will meet?

APPENDIX
WITH JOBSEEKERS IN MIND

Professions/Industries Encountered Along the Journey

Accounting
Airline
Architectural Design
Baking
Banking
Cable Television
Car Rental
Car Sales
Cellular Service
Childcare
Civil Engineering
Coaching
Commercial
Development
Construction
Cosmetic
Counseling, Retirement
Dental
Economist
Education
Electrical Engineering
Electrician
Energy
Family Medicine
Finance
Fitness
Food and Beverage

Foster care/Adoption
Grocery
Healthcare
Healthy Foods
Home Décor Retail
Home Staging
Hospitality
Insurance
Information Technology
Landscape Architecture
Legal
Librarian
Loan Officer
Marketing
Marital Arts
Mechanical Engineering
Medical Device Sales
Ministry
Mortgage
Movie Production
Music
Nonprofits
Notary
Nursing
Occupational Therapy
Office Administration
Oil & Gas

Orthodontic Care
Outdoor Recreation
Pet/House Sitting
Politics
Postal Service
Public Safety
Public Speaking
Ranching
Real Estate
Recruiting
Remodeling
Retail Management
Restaurant Business
School Administration
Security Systems
Social Media
Speech-Language
Pathology
Therapeutic Massage
Videography/Editing
Women's Ministry
Washer/Dryer -
International Sales
Zipline/Obstacle Course
Design

Appendix with Jobseekers in Mind (cont.)

Finding the Hidden Job Market

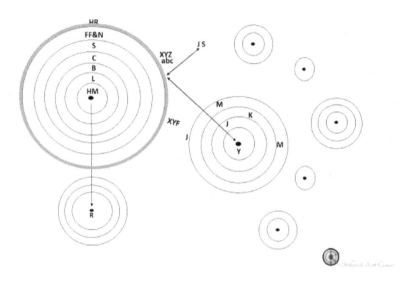

Looking for a keynote speaker or someone to speak to your
business or organization?
Kymberli knows the importance of bringing in a speaker that can
connect to your audience and deliver content that impacts. She
is passionate about bringing substance, not fluff. She is easy to
work with and will target her message to meet the needs of your
audience or business.
Contact Kymberli to begin a conversation on how she can help.
KymberliSpeight.com
kymberlispeight@gmail.com

ABOUT THE AUTHOR

Kymberli Speight's motto is "Be proactive! Enhance your brand to reach your target audience." She is a keynote speaker, an executive coach, and a Certified Professional Career Coach (CPCC), who has worked with separating active duty military executives and civilian clients transitioning to their next career opportunity. She leverages her networking expertise to teach viable skills necessary for making a successful transition. Kymberli is certified at the master's level with the Reach personal branding process and holds additional certifications in Conversational Intelligence, and 360 Reach.

Prior to coaching, Kymberli developed futures. She was also an executive recruiter for Zingaro & Company in the life science and healthcare industry. Additionally, Kymberli worked for the Vice President of Client Services at Catapult Health, a start-up company, with initial staffing and training. Kymberli has a strong background in contract negotiations. Her claim to fame is that she once spent $954M. As an active duty officer, she was the buyer for the fiscal year 1991 annual year buy of the Air Force's F-15E fighter jet.

Kymberli has a desire for helping military members make a smooth transition into the civilian sector. Moving every 2-3 years herself in support of the Air Force mission and observing the transition process as the spouse of a retired Air Force Colonel gives her firsthand experience with the complexity of transition. She now facilitates the Executive Transition Assistance Program (ETAP) at several Air Force Bases across the US. In addition to working with the military, Kymberli considers it a privilege to have served in the Air Force for 5 years active duty and 6 years in the reserves after graduating from the Air Force Academy.

Kymberli is passionate about giving back to the communities that have helped shape her personal and professional life. She delivers content loaded keynotes on networking (relationship building) and enhancing your personal brand (your reputation) as well as inspirational topics. When she is not working, Kymberli enjoys traveling and spending time with family and friends.

CPSIA information can be obtained
at www.ICGtesting.com
Printed in the USA
FSHW011819240120